THE JAGUAR

Look for these and other books in the
Lucent Endangered Animals and Habitats series:

The Amazon Rain Forest
The Bald Eagle
The Bear
Birds of Prey
Coral Reefs
The Cougar
The Elephant
The Giant Panda
The Gorilla
The Jaguar
The Manatee
The Oceans
The Orangutan
The Rhinoceros
Seals and Sea Lions
The Shark
Snakes
The Tiger
Turtles and Tortoises
The Whale
The Wolf

Other related titles in the Lucent Overview series:

Acid Rain
Endangered Species
Energy Alternatives
Garbage
The Greenhouse Effect
Hazardous Waste
Ocean Pollution
Oil Spills
Ozone
Pesticides
Population
Rainforests
Recycling
Saving the American Wilderness
Vanishing Wetlands
Zoos

THE JAGUAR

BY ANN MALASPINA

Endangered Animals & Habitats

LUCENT BOOKS, INC.
SAN DIEGO, CALIFORNIA

LUCENT *Overview Series*

This book is dedicated to Sam and Nicholas, who inspired me with their many questions about the jaguar.

Library of Congress Cataloging-in-Publication Data

Malaspina, Ann, 1957–
  The jaguar / by Ann Malaspina.
    p. cm. — (Endangered animals & habitats)
Includes bibliographical references and index.
  ISBN 1-56006-813-2 (hardcover : alk. paper)
  1. Jaguar—Juvenile literature. 2. Endangered species—Juvenile
literature. [1. Jaguar. 2. Endangered species.] I. Title. II. Series.
  QL737.C23 M25 2001
  599.75'5—dc21
                                          00-010095

Copyright © 2001 by Lucent Books, Inc.
P.O. Box 289011, San Diego, CA 92198-9011
Printed in the U.S.A.

Contents

Introduction

JAGUARS WANDER FREELY in the thick underbrush of the Cockscomb Basin Wildlife Sanctuary in Belize, the only jaguar preserve in the world, located in a mountainous tropical rain forest in the northeastern corner of Central America. But visitors to the preserve, which is open to the public, should not expect to actually see the golden cat with black spots, even in this protected region where jaguars are not threatened by hunters, poachers, loggers, or vanishing habitat. "They are there, of course, but the chances of seeing one is about seventeen thousand to one,"[1] warns a statement on the preserve's website.

Few tourists, or even animal biologists, ever actually see the jaguar in its preferred natural home, the dense tropical rain forests of Latin America, where its dappled fur merges with the shadows of leaves and trees. Forest dweller and nocturnal hunter, the jaguar, called by some the "King of Darkness," easily eludes human encounters. Instead, people may glimpse the jaguar's pugmarks, or footprints, along muddy stretches of forest trails, or hear the grunt that is the jaguar's roar, or find the remains of an armadillo, one of the cat's favorite prey.

The jaguar was revered by the native civilizations of Latin America. Perceived as a kind of god, a symbol of power and darkness, the jaguar was both admired and feared by the Indians who shared its forest. The Mayans believed the jaguar was a companion in the spiritual world, a link to the world of the dead. Intricate jade statues of creatures that were half man and half jaguar were left behind by the ancient Olmecs of Mexico. The Aztecs, whose best warriors wore the skin of the jaguar, believed the wild cat's eyes were mirrors to the human soul.

When the Spanish explorer Hernando Cortez entered the Aztec capital of Tenochtitlán in 1519, he discovered a zoo behind the Aztec leader Montezuma's palace. The zoo was filled with armadillos, sloths, monkeys, pumas, and jaguars held in bronze cages. The Europeans had never before seen the big cat, which only exists in the Americas, and they later freed the jaguars and other animals.

With the European conquest of the New World, the jaguar's status in the cultural life of Latin America, and its safety in remote jungles, was lost. The Indians were forced to give up their religions and cultures, and the worship of the jaguar ended, at least formally. More critically, hunting of the jaguar increased, and its habitat began to disappear. According to jaguar historian Richard Perry, in the early years of the Spanish conquest, two thousand jaguars were killed annually in the valley of the La Plata River in Paraguay. By the early twentieth century, cattle ranchers had virtually exterminated jaguars in Uruguay.

Today, the jaguar's future is increasingly uncertain as Latin America undergoes new waves of development and population expansion. Deforestation, conversion of jaguar habitat to other uses, and the killing of jaguars and their prey stand as the major threats to the wild cat. In a shrinking, fragmented range of tropical rain forests, swampy grasslands, and arid forests, stretching from Mexico to northern Argentina, the jaguar struggles to hold on. Only in the Amazon Basin, part of Venezuela, Guyana, Suriname, and French Guiana are jaguar populations

The Mayans, who believed that the jaguar was a link to the spirit world, carved this jaguar adorning the Pyramid of the Jaguar in Teotihuacan, Mexico.

possibly stabilized or increasing, according to the American Zoo and Aquarium Association.

Yet even as its numbers diminish, the jaguar retains its position as the only big cat in the Western Hemisphere, a top predator with no rivals in the animal world. Researchers at the Wildlife Conservation Society in New York City call the jaguar a landscape or keystone species. That means the jaguar can live in a variety of habitats and, like other large animals who hunt prey, can help regulate the numbers of reptiles, birds, mammals, and insects. The prey in turn impact the plants and other animals in the region. Thus, the biodiversity of the entire ecosystem is indirectly shaped by the presence of a jaguar; once it disappears, the ecosystem starts to collapse.

Some of the cat's battles for survival have already been won, at least on paper. In the twentieth century, the jaguar was hunted by sportsmen and fur traders, who nearly extinguished the cat by the 1960s. National and international laws

Secretive jaguars prefer to live in dense tropical forests.

now protect the jaguar from sport hunting and trade. In fact, jaguars are legally protected over much of their range, although researchers with the Wildlife Conservation Society have found that the laws are not adequately enforced.

Still, jaguars today are being forced to live perilously close to people. Logging, agriculture, ranching, and urbanization are breaking up, and sometimes destroying, the jaguar's primary habitat, the rain forests of the Amazon River Basin and other once-remote forests and grasslands. As human populations press ever deeper into the jaguar's range, the cat loses not only its habitat but the prey it needs to survive.

Making the jaguar's rescue difficult is the fact that the animal is hard to study in the wild. Unlike lions who lie out on wide-open African savannas, jaguars prefer closed tropical forests, where they live solitary, secretive, and nocturnal lives. Sometimes called the "Phantom of the Jungle," the jaguar is distinctive for how little is known about it. Zoos house fewer jaguars than lions, tigers, and leopards, and studies of the jaguar are scarce. When documentary filmmakers Carol and Richard Foster set out to film the jaguar for their PBS documentary, "Jaguar: Year of the Cat," they were able to film only captive jaguars. "Jaguars are so elusive that only a handful of wild ones have ever been photographed,"[2] Carol Foster told *E Magazine*.

Scientists have only begun to count the jaguars and find out where they still live. They do know, however, that most jaguars share their habitat, whether a national park in Belize or a Brazilian cattle ranch, to some extent with humans, an uneasy alliance for both. Thus, the question looming largest for jaguars is whether the big cat and human civilization can continue to share the earth.

1

The Jaguar and Its Behavior

IN THE DARK of the night, the jaguar springs from its sturdy back legs to snatch and kill an armadillo on the floor of a rain forest in Belize. From atop a tree overlooking a tributary of the Amazon River in Peru, the jaguar waits patiently, then plunges into the water to sink its teeth into the brittle shell of a tortoise. Using its excellent vision, agility, and coordination, the jaguar skillfully stalks and kills a deer on an open grassland in Brazil.

The name *jaguar* probably comes from the pre-Colombian South American Indian word *yaguar*, meaning "he who kills with one leap" or "a beast that kills its prey with one bound." The scientific name of the jaguar is *Panthera onca*. *Panthera* is Greek, meaning "hunter," while *onca* is Greek for "hook" or "barb," referring to the jaguar's claws. Both terms are good descriptions of this adept hunter, since the jaguar is the most powerful hunter in its range and its claws are important tools for catching prey.

The jaguar has the sharp teeth, gripping claws, strong jaw, and nimble body befitting its regal status as the top predator in the Western Hemisphere. Like all cats, the jaguar can intently focus its attention on its prey. Its padded feet make no noise on the forest floor, and the jaguar will not pounce until it nears its prey. While not especially fast or large, the jaguar, with its strong biting muscles and sturdy pointed canine teeth, is thought to have the most lethal bite of any big cat. In fact, the jaguar's only living predator is a human with a firearm.

Evolution of the jaguar

The jaguar is a mammal and belongs to the family Felidae, a group that includes thirty-seven species of wild and domestic cats. Its closest relatives are the three other big cats in the genus *Panthera*—the lion, leopard, and tiger. The four cats are distinguished from all other cats by their ability to roar and to attack prey by stalking, leaping, and killing with a bite to the neck or skull. The cheetah, snow leopard, and puma are sometimes considered big cats, but they belong to separate genuses. About 2 million years ago, the jaguar emerged in Eurasia, along with its close cousin the leopard, but the jaguar left the leopard behind to migrate over the Bering land bridge to North America. The only other big cat in North America was the American lion, but it became extinct during the last Ice Age, about eleven thousand years ago.

While similar to its modern counterpart, the prehistoric jaguar was larger, heavier, and had longer legs. That jaguar developed into many subspecies, some of which are probably now extinct. Scientists have identified five to eight modern jaguar subspecies, varying only slightly from each other, which have adapted to different climates, terrains, and food sources in scattered regions of Mexico, and Central and

The jaguar is a member of the genus Panthera, *which also includes the lion, leopard, and tiger.*

South America. However, ongoing studies of jaguar DNA may lead scientists to conclude that there are actually fewer subspecies today.

While capable of surviving in many different habitats, the jaguar is primarily a rain forest cat, wandering and hunting in low-lying wet habitats, such as swampy savannas or forests alongside rivers. "Nearly all jaguar trails lead to rivers, and it is islands, rivers, marsh and swamp that are the normal haunts of jaguars . . . because these are also the haunts of their prey,"[3] writes Richard Perry in his classic book *The World of the Jaguar*. However, the adaptable jaguar has been found high in Costa Rican mountains, in the arid Chaco forests of Paraguay and Bolivia, and in the dry mountainous borderlands of Mexico and the United States.

Physical characteristics

The adaptability of the cat is probably greatly due to its physical characteristics, which enable it to hunt successfully in a wide variety of environments. The jaguar is distinguished from the other big cats by its short, stocky legs and broad footpads. Like all cats, the jaguar's forefeet have five toes and the hind feet have four. The jaguar is digitigrade; that is, it walks on its toes with the back part of the foot raised. Its sharp claws are retractable. The cat pulls them in so that they do not scratch or rip, until it is necessary.

Medium-sized for a big cat, the jaguar is smaller than the tiger and the lion but larger than the leopard. The jaguar's length can stretch to six feet, with a tail length of about twenty-seven inches. Adult jaguars weigh between 124 and 211 pounds, with larger individuals weighing up to 333 pounds, according to the Wildlife Conservation Society. Females are 10 to 20 percent smaller than males. After former U.S. president Theodore Roosevelt first saw a jaguar in Brazil in 1913, he described it with awe: "It was a big, powerfully built creature, giving the same effect of strength that a tiger or lion does, and that the lithe leopards and pumas do not."[4]

The individual jaguar's size varies according to its diet and territory. The largest jaguars are found in the Pan-

Leopards and Jaguars

Because their size and coloring are similar, jaguars and leopards are often confused. In fact, the two big cats most likely shared the same prehistoric ancestor. The leopard also has black spots, but the jaguar's dark rosettes actually contain smaller black spots. Another difference between the two is that the leopard is found in sub-Saharan Africa and Asia, while the jaguar lives only in Central and South America, and occasionally in the southwestern United States.

The jaguar is actually larger, heavier, and less graceful than the leopard. The jaguar has a broader head, shorter, thicker legs, and a shorter tail. But there are similarities between the two cats. For instance, the jaguar and leopard are both very adaptable when it comes to habitat and prey. Even more so than the jaguar, the leopard can live almost anywhere—in forests, swamps, and even semideserts and mountains. It feeds on a wide range of prey, from reptiles to large birds, rodents to fish.

Because the leopard is so versatile—and is even able to live without water for long periods—it has survived more successfully in many regions than the other big cats, although some of its subspecies, such as the Amur leopard in tropical Asia, are endangered. Trophy hunting of leopards is still allowed in many countries. While international laws prohibit trade in the leopard, illegal smuggling of leopard pelts and bones for traditional medicine and disappearing habitat and persecution by livestock owners present the most serious risks to the leopard's future.

tanal—the sprawling lowland plains that flank Brazil's border with Bolivia and Paraguay—where they catch and eat big prey such as cattle and deer in the seasonally flooded grasslands. In 1989, Brazilian safari organizer Tony de Almeida took hunters to a remote region in the Bolivian Pantanal where an isolated rancher had been suffering from jaguar attacks on his cattle. There, he shot two jaguars whose skulls were the largest ever recorded.

However, in places such as the rain forests of Belize, where prey is smaller and more plentiful, jaguars do not need to roam so far to find food and tend to be smaller.

With its compact body, the jaguar is not one of the fastest cats. But it has other qualities that allow it to maneuver equally well on land, in water, or in trees. Having a cat's flexible spine, the jaguar is skillful at many activities necessary for hunting, including leaping, climbing, running, and swimming. Ernesto Saqui, a Mayan Indian who managed the world's only jaguar refuge in Belize, once described the jaguar to a visiting reporter as "the most graceful creature alive."[5]

Eyes, ears, and whiskers

Assisting the jaguar in the hunt are its excellent sensory organs, including its eyes, ears, and whiskers. The jaguar's eyes, with golden yellow to pale-green yellow irises, are sensitive to light and allow the big cat to hunt in the dimness of twilight and even at night. In sunlight, the pupils contract to prevent glare, becoming circular dots. At night, the jaguar's pupils open wide to gather as much light as they can. The jaguar has a mirror-like tissue, called the tapetum lucidum, behind the retina. When light passes through the retina, this tissue reflects the light back, providing additional stimulation to the retina's light receptors and enhancing the cat's vision. Also, jaguars' eyes face forward, allowing for overlapping vision and providing good depth perception. Thus, jaguars can accurately judge distances and the size of objects.

Jaguars, like all cats, have an acute sense of hearing. The cat has relatively small, short, rounded ears, with black back sides and white central spots. Their external ears, or pinnae, are very mobile and have twenty muscles to move them. The cup-shaped pinnae capture sound waves and direct them to the middle and inner ear. By turning their ears toward a sound, jaguars can pinpoint its source.

The jaguar's whiskers are another important sensory organ. Cats' whiskers, or vibrissae, contain a plentiful nerve supply that enables them to sense the slightest movement or touch, signaling danger or opportunity. At night, the jaguar's whiskers help it maneuver through thick brush and avoid low branches.

Spotted cat

Although the jaguar's excellent sensory organs are similar to those of other cats, its spotted fur is distinctive. According to one Indian myth, the jaguar got its markings by dabbing mud on its body with its paws. The jaguar's fur is usually a rich shade of pale gold to rusty red with black spots, with a whitish shade on its stomach. What appears to be the jaguar's spots are actually large broken-edge rosettes, or circles, which enclose smaller black spots. The jaguar's tail is also spotted, with black stripes at its tip.

Some jaguars are melanistic, or all black, but even black jaguars have dark rosettes. Some Indians believed that black jaguars were bigger and more powerful than spotted jaguars, but actually the jaguars are identical except for their coats. If a spotted jaguar and black jaguar mate, the female may give birth to twin cubs, one black and one spotted.

The jaguar's distinctive spotted fur is usually a shade of pale gold to rusty red with black spots.

The melanistic, or all-black, jaguar and the spotted jaguar have different coat colors, but they are otherwise identical.

The roar

The most distinguishing characteristics of the four big cats, including the jaguar, are the ability to roar and the lack of a purr. Yet the jaguar's roar is different from the loud roar of the lion and tiger. Some people say jaguars do not roar but, rather, signal each other with a repeated series of deep grunts. L. H. Emmons, writing in *The Smithsonian Book of North American Mammals*, describes the jaguar's roar as "a bow being rasped across the strings of a bass fiddle."[6] Others say the jaguar's roar is distinctive and unforgettable: "And then I hear it. A roar. Deep. Resonant. Close. The sound stops. The jungle is quiet. Whatever it was has slipped away, perhaps to stalk a straggling pig, or perhaps to venture beneath the surface of this world, on the hunt for those spirits that would otherwise vex the day,"[7] writes one travel writer who listened for the jaguar in Belize.

Jaguar, the hunter

Combined, the jaguar's physical characteristics make it a notoriously efficient hunter. In 1848, British naturalist

Henry Walter Bates was traveling the Upper Amazon in Brazil when he discovered the remains of an alligator. "The head, forequarters, and bony shell were the only parts which remained, but the meat was quite fresh, and there were many footmarks of the jaguar around the carcass; so that there was no doubt that this had formed the solid part of the animal's breakfast,"[8] he wrote.

When hungry, the jaguar will comb trees for sloths and monkeys or plunge into rivers after fish and turtles. However, the cat primarily hunts on the ground, walking stealthily along trails or beside rivers and streams. Often it wades in the water to scoop up fish with one powerful paw. On land, the jaguar is able to creep low to the ground to stalk its prey.

When a jaguar spots prey, it quietly follows the animal and then, at an opportune moment and with explosive

 ## The Coat of the Jaguar

The jaguar's spotted coat serves many purposes for this wilderness survivor. Perhaps most important, the jaguar's fur helps camouflage, or hide, the cat as it tracks its prey through the shadowy light of the rain forest. The jaguar's irregular pattern of dark spots and blotches merges with the dim, changing color patterns on the forest floor and allows the cat to sneak up on its prey. Some scientists believe the jaguar's color may vary depending on the habitat. Jaguars who dwell in rain forests may be darker than those who live on open grassland and in scrub forest, since a darker coat merges better with the low light of thick jungle.

But camouflage is not the only purpose of the jaguar's fur. It also protects the cat's skin from being scratched and damaged by the rough daily life of a hunter. The distinctive spotted top coat has long, strong guard hairs. Next to the skin is an undercoat of short, wooly fur. Besides offering protection, the fur emits scent messages to attract potential mates and warn intruders that the cat's territory is already claimed.

A jaguar will enter a pond or river to hunt, but it primarily hunts on the ground.

power and energy, the cat leaps. Although the jaguar's long, sharp claws are usually covered in a sheath, the claws emerge at the moment it strikes. With its claws thus extended, or protracted, the cat holds its prey in a powerful grip. It is difficult, if not impossible, to escape the grasp of the jaguar. As Dale Anderson, who heads the Sierra Endangered Cat Haven in California, described the cat, "The jaguar is the pit bull of the cat species."[9]

The jaguar has different methods of killing, depending on the size of the prey. The cat kills small animals just by slapping them with a paw, so that the animal dies of skull injuries. When it attacks larger mammals, such as deer, the jaguar wrestles its victim down and bites the head or neck. The jaguar is the only big cat that frequently kills by piercing the prey's skull with its sharp canine teeth. Scientists believe this is because the water-loving jaguar has adapted to preying on hard-shelled reptiles, such as turtles. Jaguars use their canine teeth to pierce the shells of tortoises, armadillos, and other hard-shelled animals. They break apart the top of the shell, then scoop out the meat with their paws.

One of the world's leading jaguar experts, Alan Rabinowitz, director of the Global Carnivore Program at the Wildlife Conservation Society, studied jaguars in Belize from 1984 to 1986. One day he came upon the remains of a peccary, a kind of wild pig, the skull separated from the rest of the skeleton. After examining the skull, he was sure the peccary had been killed by a jaguar. "I saw that the top of the cranium was missing like a piece of a puzzle. Only one animal in this part of the world had the power to do that," he wrote. "As I had seen repeatedly, the killing power of a jaguar was awesome."[10]

Diet

Since its strength and agility allow it to attack prey of any size, even those larger than itself, the jaguar will eat just about any animal. Scientists believe the jaguar eats as many as eighty-five species, depending on which animals share its territory. "They're very adaptable predators," says biologist Brian Miller of the Denver Zoo. "They can live in many different habitats and eat many different types of prey."[11]

In Belize, Rabinowitz collected and studied jaguar droppings to find out what the cats eat. About 50 percent of the diet appeared to be armadillos, an animal plentiful in the area, with another large portion consisting of deer. Scientists in the dry Chaco region of Paraguay in the late 1980s found that jaguars there ate gray brocket deer, rabbits, armadillos, peccaries, and salt desert cavies, or wild guinea pigs.

The jaguar will attack large and small mammals, such as tapirs, peccaries, porcupines, otters, sloths, capybaras (the largest living rodents), armadillos, monkeys, skunks, and coatis (fur-bearing animals with long tails and snouts). Reptiles, too, are fare for the jaguar, including snakes, iguanas, and caimans (a relative of the alligator), as well as turtles and tortoises. If they can catch them, jaguars will eat birds such as herons, storks, anhingas, cormorants, and curassows.

When jaguars live near farms or ranches, as they do in the grasslands of the Pantanal and the cleared Chaco forests of Paraguay, they may attack and eat horses, cattle, or other livestock, although some jaguar experts say these attacks occur less frequently than some people believe. However, the problem of jaguars sharing land with livestock is a serious one, for farmers and ranchers shoot jaguars that threaten their livelihood. "They are still perceived as varmints that compete with humans for wildlife, and that may prey on livestock, so many are killed on sight,"[12] says Carlos Lopez Gonzales, a researcher at the Instituto de Ecologia in Veracruz, Mexico.

Jaguar, man-eaters?

One species not usually found in the jaguar's varied diet is the human species. Tigers, lions, and leopards have reputations as man-eaters, but there have been only rare reports of jaguar attacks on people in recent years. However, historians of the big cat in Central and South America have found anecdotal accounts of jaguars who did indeed kill and eat people. In *The World of the Jaguar*, Perry recounts stories of jaguars approaching campfires or tracking people through forests, but he acknowledges that the cases of jaguars attacking humans are not well documented. Wildlife scientists today generally agree that jaguars do not attack people unless there is an accidental close encounter—or the animal is sick or desperate for food.

Nonetheless, people should not invite contact with a jaguar. In *Jaguar: One Man's Struggle to Establish the World's First Jaguar Preserve*, Rabinowitz recounts his

Most wildlife scientists agree that jaguars will not attack a human being unless there is an accidental encounter or the animal is desperate for food.

experience with a young jaguar he had been studying, which ended with the jaguar nearly killing him. Wildlife ecologist Anne LaBastille tells of allowing a young jaguar, raised from birth in a rustic safari park in Panama, to grab her leg and climb up her back. She writes, "I could feel the tremendous power in her jaws and paws. That taut, gorgeous, black-and-gold body was lithe and muscular. If she wanted to, she could snap my neck like a straw or rip my jugular like paper. . . . Suddenly I felt afraid."[13]

Tracking the jaguar

Like most people, LaBastille saw the jaguar in captivity, for it is rare to sight the jaguar in the wild. Wide-ranging and mostly nocturnal, the jaguar is difficult to spot and track in the rain forest. Until the use of radio collars, or radiotelemetry, was developed in the 1970s, scientists were not able to follow jaguars in the wild. Using this method, scientists shoot the jaguars with tranquilizers to temporarily sedate them, fit them with light collars with radio transmitters, and release them. Scientists can then use receivers and antennas to track the cats' movements and habits, and sometimes recapture them at a later date.

Camera traps are also used to study jaguars. Researchers place self-operated cameras with small infrared beams along trails. When a movement breaks the electronic beam, the shutter-release trips, taking a picture and allowing scientists to count the jaguars and prey animals that use the trail. Researchers also study jaguar tracks to find out about their movements and population density.

Using radiotelemetry to follow jaguars' movements day and night through the forest, researcher Rabinowitz learned a lot about the jaguars' territories in the Cockscomb Basin. "When we could follow the same male jaguars on consecutive days, we saw that, despite the size of their overall range, the jaguars would often stay within a square mile area for about a week before shifting, in a single night, to another part of their range,"[14] he wrote. He was also able to estimate how many jaguars lived in a certain area.

Territorial animals

As Rabinowitz learned, jaguars are territorial, meaning that each cat designates an area in which to live and hunt. A jaguar marks out its territory by scratching trees and logs and leaving droppings in the middle of trails. The jaguars also leave their scent, excreted from glands on the muzzle and temples and behind the tail. Within their territories, jaguars usually live alone.

The size of a jaguar's territory varies according to the prey. Jaguars can remain in one place, within a circular territory of three square miles, for a long time, but if they need to find food, they may claim a territory of two hundred square miles, and they have been known to travel as far as five hundred miles for food. Territories may be smaller in the rain forest, where prey is more plentiful, and larger in habitats where food is scarce. In the Brazilian Pantanal, scientists found that home areas of jaguars were smaller in the wet season and larger in dry months, when the cats had to search farther for food.

Because they are larger and eat more, male jaguars need twice as much territory as females. Each male has a territory that overlaps with the ranges of several females, according to one source. Sometimes even male jaguars have overlapping ranges if there is adequate prey, but

Jaguars usually live alone within territories that vary in size depending on the proximity of prey.

they still keep out of each other's way, says biologist Miller. "They seem to work things out so that when one is in one part of the home range, another individual is in another part,"[15] says Miller.

Mating, gestation, and birth

The usually solitary jaguar seeks out other jaguars only when it wants to mate. Jaguars of both sexes emit roaring calls and leave urinary scent markings to signal they are ready to mate; these help males locate receptive and fertile females. Scientists believe that jaguars do not have a particular mating season in the tropics, where the climate does not change much year-round, although the best time to give birth is in the rainy season because prey is more abundant. Researcher Rabinowitz observed that jaguars in Belize tended to mate in the late winter and give birth between May and September, during the rainy season.

After mating, the pair separates, and only the female will care for the offspring. A jaguar pregnancy, or gestation, lasts about 90 to 105 days. To ensure the safety of her kittens, the mother jaguar seeks a protective shelter of rocks, trees, or bushes where she will give birth. A mother jaguar may give birth to between one and four kittens, but two are most common.

When they are born, the kittens are covered with long, wooly pale fur, heavily marked with black spots and black stripes on their faces. After eleven to thirteen days, they open their eyes. They don't begin to walk until they are about eighteen days old. When they reach about six weeks, the jaguar kittens start following their mother on her forays for food and water.

Learning by imitation

In their first weeks, the jaguars get their nourishment solely from their mother's milk. The kittens begin eating solid food, brought to them by their mother, when they are seventy days old. After about four to five months, the mother weans her young, but they stay with her until they are two years old. During this time, young jaguars

Jaguar cubs learn survival skills by imitating their mother's behavior.

learn to hunt and survive in the wild by copying their mother's behavior. She may bring them half-killed prey and let them try swatting and killing it themselves. Chasing each other's tails and wrestling playfully helps the young jaguars practice their predatory skills.

Jaguars attain full size and sexual maturity at two to three years for females and three to four years for males. The young jaguars then set out and mark their own territory. If all goes well, they can look forward to a relatively long life. Captive jaguars have been known to live for up to twenty-two years. However, jaguars in the wild probably live only half as long.

Jaguar survival

The jaguar's physical features and abilities that make it a superior hunter have enabled it to survive for thousands of years. Its capacity to live in a variety of environments, as long as prey is plentiful, has kept it alive while other prehistoric animals, which once shared the earth with the jaguar, have disappeared. Thus, the cat known in much of Latin America as El Tigre, or "The Tiger," still roams some of its ancient hunting grounds, even while the human civilizations that once revered the animal have long since vanished.

2

Hunting the Jaguar

HUNTING THE JAGUAR for sport and profit, and to protect livestock from predation nearly wiped out the cat during the twentieth century. For many decades, the jaguar was a moving target to be shot and killed, if possible. The spotted skin of the jaguar was considered a sports trophy or a profit-making commodity. Little consideration was given to protecting the jaguar, for people did not yet recognize, or they were unconcerned, that the big cat, solitary and slow to reproduce, would become endangered with over-hunting. By the 1960s and 1970s, the jaguar population was seriously depleted.

The jaguar hunt

U.S. President Theodore Roosevelt was one of many hunters who traveled deep into the swamps and jungles of South America for the thrill of a jaguar hunt. In late December 1913, Roosevelt tracked a jaguar before dawn, the sky lit by the Southern Cross constellation, in a swamp near the headwaters of the Paraguay River in Brazil. Led by professional jaguar hunters, Indians, and a pack of hounds, Roosevelt chased a jaguar into a tree. "We saw the jaguar high among the forked limbs of a taruman tree. It was a beautiful picture—the spotted coat of the big, lithe, formidable cat fairly shone as it snarled defiance at the pack below." Roosevelt fired once with his Springfield rifle: "The jaguar fell like a sack of sand through the branches, and although it staggered to its feet it went but a score of yards before it sank down, and when I came up it

U.S. president Theodore Roosevelt poses with a jaguar he killed during a South American hunting trip in 1913.

was dead under the palms, with three or four of the bolder dogs riving at it." Tracking the big cat was the ultimate South American adventure for Roosevelt, who had already hunted cougars in the Rockies and lions in Africa. "The jaguar is the king of South American game, ranking on an equality with the noblest beasts of the chase of America,"[16] he wrote.

Until the 1970s, jaguar hunting was a popular and legal sport for wealthy international trophy hunters. Professional jaguar hunters, assisted by local Indians, or *tigreros*, who knew the terrain and habits of the jaguar, led sportsmen through the jungles and swamps of Central and South America in search of the elusive, nocturnal cat. Safari leaders charged thousands of dollars to take tourists into the most remote regions of Brazil, Venezuela, Belize, and other countries to search for the jaguar. The grasslands of the Brazilian Pantanal, where the world's largest jaguars roamed in plentiful numbers, was a popular hunting ground. British Honduras, now Belize, with its rugged, damp jungle terrain housing a significant jaguar population, was also a destination of choice for jaguar hunters.

Legendary jaguar hunters included the Brazilian Tony de Almeida, who chronicled his colorful hunting career in, *Jaguar Hunting in the Matto-Gross and Bolivia: With*

Notes on Other Game. In the 1930s, American adventurer Sasha Siemel killed jaguars mostly on ranches in Brazil, where he described them as "murderous killers" who had to be destroyed to protect cattle. "There is little room, of course, for sentimentality with a charging *tigre*. Yet I felt no elation at killing the animal," Siemel wrote about killing his first jaguar. "Something in the calm, almost regal disdain of that first *tigre* . . . has made it impossible for me ever to regard this lonely lord of the jungle with anything but the deepest respect."[17] Siemel reported that he killed three hundred jaguars in his time, some with a spear.

Hunting jaguars took persistence, as well as knowledge of the terrain and the habits of the cat. To lure the cats out into the open, jaguar hunters used drum-like instruments known as jaguar callers, which imitate the jaguar's gravelly roar. In *Jaguar,* Alan Rabinowitz describes a jaguar caller made from a large gourd covered on one side with deerskin. A jaguar hunter showed Rabinowitz how to use it. The Indian rubbed a piece of banana peel, hardened with beeswax and hanging inside the gourd, to imitate the deep grunt of a jaguar. In his travels in Belize, Rabinowitz also saw jaguar callers made of plastic milk jugs

American adventurer Sasha Siemel (pictured) said that he always had a deep respect for the many jaguars he killed in Brazil.

and cardboard boxes. He noticed that these devices made it quite easy to attract jaguars, which were curious about the sound.

On the trail for jaguars, hunters often look for jaguar tracks and feces or broken twigs and branches where the jaguar might have rested. They also look for fresh kills, since the jaguar might be close by. Jaguar hunters often use dogs specially trained to follow the big cat's scent. The dogs, each accompanied by a handler, track the jaguars and chase them into trees, where they are easy targets for the hunter's gun.

Indians traditionally hunted jaguars with spears, knives, sticks, and bows and arrows, but in the years following World War I, guns became the jaguar hunter's preferred weapon. The ease with which jaguars could be killed with guns accelerated the hunting of the cats. Eventually, however, many countries recognized that sport hunting posed a significant threat to the big cat and passed laws banning the activity. Today, jaguar hunting for sport is prohibited in most countries, though the laws are not always enforced.

The fur trade

While some jaguar hunters tracked the cat for sport, others did so for profit. From the early 1900s to the 1970s, jaguars were hunted in large numbers for their pelts. The fur trade peaked during the 1960s and 1970s, when the fur of jaguars and other wild spotted cats was in great demand and widely sold in high-priced fur stores and fashion boutiques around the world.

For people willing to pay the price, a coat made from the pelt of a jaguar was for many years considered a symbol of wealth, beauty, and power. A glamorous Sophia Loren, then one of the world's most popular film stars, was photographed on a New York City street in a full-length jaguar coat. First Lady Jackie Kennedy, considered one of the most stylish women of her time, liked to wear a leopard coat.

Because jaguars and other wild cats were hunted in the wild, rather than raised on fur farms, their pelts brought substantial sums to the traders. A single jaguar pelt could be sold for as much as $20,000 and this potential for large profits ignited the industry. Around eighteen thousand jaguars were killed every year for their fur in the 1960s and 1970s, according to one source. The Wildlife Conservation Society reports that over twenty-three thousand jaguar skins were imported into the United States in 1967 and 1968; and, in the late 1960s, fifteen thousand jaguars were being shot each year in the Brazilian Amazon rain forest. Brazil exported over 104,400 pounds of jaguar skins in 1969, according to one report. "Probably twice as many skins were taken as were reported because hides were often inadequately skinned, stored, or tanned, resulting in having to discard those skins as unsuitable,"[18] writes Tom Brakefield in *Big Cats*. A photograph in *National Geographic* in 1972, shows a warehouse in Manaus, Brazil, in the Central Amazon, piled high with the skins of jaguars, ocelots, and margays, two other wild cats.

The popularity of clothing made from jaguar pelts peaked in the 1960s and 1970s when many people considered the clothing to be a symbol of wealth, beauty, and power.

Many countries were involved in the fur trade, including Brazil, Paraguay, Bolivia, Peru, and Colombia. Most of the fur exports went north, since the United States was the major market for jaguar skins, and the skins of other wild cats, up until the 1970s. Germany, and other European countries, also imported spotted cat fur from the Americas.

But as government officials and citizens began to realize that their national wildlife was being raided by poachers, traders, and furriers, they passed laws to protect their native animals, including wild cats. "The appearance of large numbers of pelts of tigers, leopards, jaguars, snow leopards and their kin in boutiques from Montevideo to New York and Berlin led to alarm that trade might drive these

species to extinction,"[19] write Kristin Nowell and Peter Jackson in *Wild Cats*. The grassroots anti-fur movement helped rally the public to stop buying goods made from wild animal pelts.

Beginning with Brazil in 1967, many Latin American countries decided to close down the trade in spotted cat fur. Brazil was followed by Venezuela, Chile, Colombia, Peru, Argentina, and the United States, all of which banned trade in wild cats, dead or alive, that were considered endangered.

Global crackdown on the fur trade

Yet individual countries alone could not stop the international trade. "Traders from these countries smuggled skins out and laundered their exports to markets abroad through other outlets,"[20] write Nowell and Jackson. Disturbed by the numbers of wild animals being killed, countries came together in 1973 to sign the Convention on International Trade in Endangered Species (CITES), which became effective two years later.

Initially signed by ten nations, CITES protects wildlife and plants from declining because of excessive trade and bans the trade of endangered species across international borders. CITES listed the jaguar in its Appendix I, meaning that the animal needed full protection and that no trade in jaguar would be tolerated by member countries. As a result, reported trade in jaguar and other big-cat skins

 Fur, Feathers, Tusks, and Big Money

Global trade in illegal animal trafficking is estimated to be a $5 billion business annually, according to the World Wide Fund for Nature (WWF). Although international laws now protect a number of plant and animal species from commercial trade, huge profits are still being made on the black market. Ecuador, Bolivia, and Brazil are among the many countries where plants and animals, including the jaguar's prey and occasionally jaguars themselves, are being stolen from wild places and sold.

Brazil's Amazon rain forest contains many rare and exotic species, and wild animal traffickers have discovered that those species translate into substantial money. In fact, wild animal trafficking, which is illegal, is estimated to bring $1 billion into Brazil each year, and many of the species affected are threatened with extinction. The rarer an animal, the more valuable it is. Through the underground trade, live animals from the rain forest wind up for sale in pet stores.

To stop this illegal trade, in 1999 the Brazilian government created RENCTAS, which is the Portuguese acronym for the National Network Against Wild Animal Traffic. A joint effort by police, nongovernmental groups, and Ibama, Brazil's federal wildlife agency, RENCTAS employs postal, police, and airlines employees to uncover smugglers. However, according to the *Miami Herald*, the traffickers who are caught pay only a nominal fine and the stolen wildlife often ends up in zoos. "No one ever goes to jail," Forest Police Major Jose Luiz Padrone told *Miami Herald* reporter Katherine Ellison. "There is no known person in jail for trafficking in animals, which certainly makes it look like Brazilian judges don't consider environmental crimes to be serious."

sharply dropped by the end of the 1970s, although illegal trade continued.

Black market trade

Even though legal hunting and international trade in threatened and endangered species was reduced by the late 1970s, illegal poaching and black market trade in wild animals remain a problem, particularly in Latin American rain forests and other remote regions where it is difficult for governments to monitor activity and enforce laws. In fact, smuggling profits usually increase once a species becomes rare or protected, which gives new incentive to poachers and traders. One researcher in Venezuela in 1997 reported that the skin of an adult jaguar may garner as much as $10,000 on the black market. In other countries, live jaguars are still occasionally bought and sold, according to scattered reports. "I've even gotten a jaguar for one man. They are in demand because they're cute when they're small,"[21] a Peruvian wildlife poacher told a reporter for the *Arizona Republic* in 1997.

While traders can no longer transport endangered species through international customs, they have less trouble selling their illegal wares in local markets. There are still occasional reports of illegal jaguar trade across borders, and probably more goes undetected. A group of Mexicans were prosecuted by the United States in 1980 for illegally importing jaguar pelts into the country. In July 1988, skins of jaguar, puma, and ocelot were among thousands of skins seized from poachers and ordered to be burned in Brazil by the Forest Police.

In 1992, the Arizona Game and Fish Department infiltrated a ring of wildlife poachers, and the following year, the federal government seized three jaguar specimens from the group, which they found had ties to Mexican jaguar hunters. They also discovered that hounds bred and trained in the United States were sold to Mexican nationals to hunt jaguars.

There have been other instances of illegal jaguar trade, as well. Two men faced five years in prison and a $250,000 fine after being convicted of illegal interstate sales of wildlife and conspiracy in 1998, according to the Associated Press. They had traveled from Arizona to New Mexico to sell a mounted jaguar and a jaguar rug, as well as a mounted ocelot and an ocelot hide, for a total of $13,000 to undercover agents in Albuquerque. Agencie EFE, a South American news agency, reported in November 1999 that jaguars and ocelots are continuing to be trafficked illegally in Bolivia and that the Bolivian government is not enforcing environmental laws.

Jaguar parts also valued

Jaguar pelts are not the only valued part of the big cat. According to the World Wide Fund for Nature (WWF), an independent wildlife conservation group, some Indians in Brazil believe that parts of the jaguar contain medicinal powers. For example, these natives use jaguar fat to cure intestinal worms, a common malady in tropical regions. Carbonized jaguar toe-

A man displays a jaguar pelt that was being sold on the black market in Brazil in 1988.

nails are used to relieve the pain of toothaches. On the black market, jaguar meat, bones, testicles, and blood are sold for use in witchcraft and for medicinal purposes, such as improving physical and mental prowess and boosting sexual performance. In Belize, Rabinowitz found that Mayan Indians collected jaguar fat to burn to keep pests away from their cornfields. In addition, jaguars still retain some of the mystique they once had in pre-Colombian cultures. The Indians make necklaces from jaguar teeth, and they spread jaguar fat on their skin to bring them courage and power.

While anecdotal evidence of jaguar poaching is available, there are no hard figures as to how many jaguars are poached annually. The numbers is probably small. But because jaguars are solitary, wide-ranging animals, the loss of a single jaguar is extremely harmful to local populations. In many regions with a jaguar presence, there are very few jaguars. Losing even one means losing the precious potential for reproduction in the future.

Controlled jaguar sport hunting

Despite concerns about dwindling jaguar populations, some hunting groups, governments, and even big-cat experts have suggested legalizing controlled trophy hunting as a way to help conserve the species. Since jaguar conservation efforts are underfunded in most countries, hunting fees could contribute to jaguar conservation and the enforcement of environmental regulations. Advocates also say that legalized sport hunting might help reduce illegal poaching and hunting and provide an economic incentive for local people to preserve jaguar habitat.

Many wildlife advocates oppose any proposal to legalize the killing of an endangered species. However, supporters of controlled hunting point out that regulated sport hunting revived some species in the United States. For instance, the white-tailed deer, nearly extinct because of unregulated overhunting in the early twentieth century, has dramatically repopulated with the imposition of controlled hunting seasons.

One proposal for controlled jaguar hunting resulted from the efforts of the Safari Club International. Collaborating with the Venezuelan government in the 1990s, this nonprofit organization of thirty-six thousand hunters proposed a plan intended to reduce both the unregulated shooting of problem jaguars and the illegal sport hunting of jaguars. "Simply because there is no legal hunting allowed, doesn't mean there's not a tremendous number of jaguars being hunted illegally,"[22] said Bill Wall, a wildlife specialist at Safari Club International. The program would have allowed the export of thirty jaguars each year as hunting trophies; only problem jaguars, which had been regularly feeding on cattle, would be the targets of the hunt. The Venezuelan Ministry of the Environment planned to use the money raised by hunting fees to finance conservation measures for the jaguar.

The proposal was opposed by the WWF, and Venezuelan wildlife advocates. "As it happens with most large cats, the

Sport Hunters Turn Researchers

Offering sport hunters a chance to participate in jaguar research is a new twist in jaguar conservation. Beginning in 1997, Safari Club International piloted a research study of jaguars in a low and dry jungle in the Calakmul Biosphere Reserve on the Yucatan Peninsula of Mexico. The project is funded in part by Safari Club members who pay a fee to participate in a nonlethal hunt of the jaguars.

Using goats to lure the jaguars, and hounds to chase the jaguars into trees, the hunters shoot the cats with darts containing tranquilizers. A veterinarian is required to be present during the capture of a jaguar. The jaguars are then fitted with radio collars, which will help the researchers track them and learn more about their movements, home range requirements, and habitat preferences. Meanwhile, the hunters come home with an experience not so different than if they had hunted the jaguar for sport, and perhaps a new commitment to saving the animal.

jaguar faces multiple threats, including habitat degradation and illegal hunting in some areas. Any proposal that would allow trade of the animals has to be approached with extreme caution because of the impact it could have on the species in the wild, not only in Venezuela but in other range countries as well,"[23] said Ginette Hemley, director of international wildlife policy at WWF-United States. Venezuelan jaguar advocates claimed the plan overestimated the jaguars' habitat and presence and, instead of conserving the species, sought to eliminate jaguars as threats to cattle and to provide sport hunters with the chance to shoot one. Ultimately, the plan did not go forward.

A long way to go

Laws prohibiting the hunting of jaguars and the trade of jaguar skins and parts have been highly successful in saving jaguars from mass killing. In some areas, after hunting was curtailed, jaguar populations apparently began to stabilize. According to a report to the National Fish and Wildlife Foundation in

1987, "jaguar numbers have begun to sustain themselves and even increase in some areas of its range as a result of loss of markets for jaguar skins brought about by CITES."[24]

However, most countries with jaguar populations do not have the funds to enforce their hunting and anti-poaching laws. Poachers usually get away with a small fine, and poached animals are often not returned to the wild but donated to zoos or wildlife parks. Even with adequate money and staff, preventing the illegal poaching of wild animals such as jaguars, especially in the remote regions where the jaguar lives, is extremely difficult.

3

Destruction of the Jaguar's Habitat: Nowhere Left to Hide

As RECENTLY AS one hundred years ago, jaguars inhabited a vast range, stretching from the southwestern United States through Mexico and Central America into Colombia, Brazil, Peru, Bolivia, Paraguay, Uruguay, and as far south as southern Argentina. But by the 1990s, the jaguar population had vanished from about 50 percent of the range it had occupied in 1900, mostly at the northern and southern edges, according to data compiled by the Wildlife Conservation Society.

No one knows how many jaguars remain in some regions, especially the southern Amazon and the Cerrado, tropical dry forests that cover one-quarter of Brazil. But the jaguar has disappeared from much of Mexico and is no longer seen in the pampas of Argentina. Coastal Brazil has lost most of its jaguars, as possibly have El Salvador, Nicaragua, Guatemala, and Uruguay, according to the World Conservation Monitoring Centre. The WWF states that the jaguar has likely been wiped out from Chile and is at risk in Argentina, Costa Rica, and Panama.

In most areas, the jaguar population has diminished because the animal's habitat has been drastically modified by human activity. As populations expanded in Latin America during the late twentieth century, trees were cleared for agriculture and cattle grazing. Roads and

highways were cut through forests, bringing people and new farms and towns. Dams, built to harness energy for electric power, flooded river plains, and logging operations leveled the rain forests. Because the jaguar needs a dense cover of forest, bush, and grass, as well as access to water and sufficient prey, the cat had fewer places to hide and hunt.

Lost jaguar land

Today, many of the jaguar's historic hunting grounds are no longer wild. In the northern part of its range, Mexico has lost at least one-third of its forest cover. On the southern edge, the native vegetation of the pampas grasslands of Argentina has been virtually eliminated by farming and ranching. In between, the swamps, dry forests, and wetlands of the Cerrado in Brazil have been planted with soybeans and other crops, pushing out native plants and animals. The Atlantic Forest, which once spread down the coast of Brazil, has nearly vanished. And now, more than ever before, the Amazon rain forest is threatened by slash-and-burn logging, new settlements, and hydroelectric dams.

Prehistoric Jaguar, History or Omen?

The current shrinking of the jaguar's range echoes a more dramatic phenomenon, which started about eleven thousand years ago. Before that, jaguars ranged over much of the continental United States, as well as Central and South America. Fossilized jaguar paw prints, dating from about 1.5 million to eleven thousand years ago, have been found in Arkansas, Washington State, Nebraska, Pennsylvania, Maryland, Tennessee, Missouri, Florida, and other states. "Jaguars were very widespread throughout North America," said Rick Toomey, curator of geology at the Illinois State Museum, in a May 2000 interview with the author. The museum's collection contains casts of jaguar footprints from sites in Tennessee and Missouri.

But something happened during the end of the last Ice Age that triggered a mass extinction. In just a few centuries, more than two-thirds of North America's large mammals became extinct. Woolly mammoths, mastodons, camels, giant ground sloths, and saber-toothed tigers disappeared forever. A close relative of the jaguar, the American lion, also became extinct in North America. Like the tapir, peccary, and llama, the jaguar did not become extinct, but its range shifted southward, primarily to Central and South America. "A variety of animals survived elsewhere, but some didn't," said Toomey.

What caused the jaguar to disappear from most of North America? One idea is that some animals could not adapt to the dramatic change in climate as temperatures rose and glaciers melted. Perhaps they could no longer find the necessary food. Or the sudden seasonal changes disrupted their mating schedules. Another factor may have been a human one. About twelve thousand years ago, people from Asia, known as the Clovis people, migrated into North America. Equipped with sharp-pointed weapons and human intuition, they hunted many of the animals that went extinct. Some scientists believe that over-hunting possibly extinguished species or that the hunting of certain important species, such as the mammoths or mastodons, led to environmental collapse.

The pressure on the jaguar's environment has quickened in recent years and poses more peril in the future, for there is no question that the loss of an animal's habitat leads directly to extinction. "The light and the way for the world's biodiversity is the preservation of natural ecosystems,"[25] writes Harvard University zoologist Edward O. Wilson. Yet just 3 to 6 percent of the jaguar range is sufficiently protected in parks or refuges, according to some estimates. For the jaguar and other large predators, time is fast running out. Saving the jaguar's habitat has become increasingly difficult.

Progress threatens jaguar habitat

That difficulty is due to the fact that progress and economic growth in Latin America, and other parts of the world, often relies on the exploitation of natural resources, which destroys wildlife habitats and puts native plants and animals at risk. For example, in the 1990s, Paraguay built a hydroelectric dam at Ayoles. The dam flooded a large island, some 486,000 acres of grasslands, displacing dozens of species of mammals, including jaguars, as well as birds and reptiles. Yet Paraguay desperately needed the electric power the plant generates.

Similarly, a gas pipeline project proposed for Bolivia may be an economic boon to the struggling South American nation, but it would imperil the jaguar and other local wildlife. The 224-mile pipeline, backed by Shell Oil, is intended to transport natural gas from Rio San Miguel in Bolivia to Cuiaba in Brazil. However, it also threatens to destroy the largest remaining tract of tropical dry forest, Kakutani Forest in eastern Bolivia, according to the WWF. Kakutani Forest is home to many endangered species, including the hyacinth macaw, maned wolf, ocelot, and jaguar. Many environmental groups oppose the pipeline.

Yet another ongoing controversy, this one in Belize, highlights the difficulty in balancing the economic and environmental needs of developing countries. The Belize government and Belize Electricity Ltd. plan to build the

Jaguars in the United States

Sometime during the first half of the twentieth century, the jaguar virtually disappeared from the United States. Breeding populations of jaguars vanished from the southwestern United States between fifty and one hundred years ago. The last record of a jaguar killed in New Mexico was 1905. Jaguars have not been killed in California since 1860, and the last record of a jaguar in Texas was in 1946. The last sightings of jaguars with young in the United States were in 1910. The cause of the jaguar's disappearance from the United States is not known, but hunting of the jaguar and its prey, and changing land uses, probably contributed to its destruction.

However, the borderlands of Mexico and the United States have served as the northern edge of the jaguar's range, and two jaguars sighted in the arid, mountainous borderlands of Mexico, Arizona, and New Mexico in 1996 raised new questions about the animal's occurrence in the southwest. Possibly these jaguars had wandered up from Mexico, where their habitat has been destroyed. No one knows for sure. Most likely they were just roaming in the United States, not breeding, since the climate and habitat are not ideal.

The sightings were significant, if only to point out that the jaguar's range is large and unpredictable, and protections for the animal may have to extend farther north than previously assumed. The Wildlife Conservation Society's Alan Rabinowitz was quoted by the Environmental News Network in 1997, saying: "With at least a few reports each decade since the late 1880s, the jaguar cannot simply be considered an accidental wanderer into the U.S. Yet the southwest has, at least in recent times, never been more than marginal habitat at the extreme northern limit of the jaguar's range."

Chalillo Dam on the Macal River to provide electricity to the country. Environmentalists oppose the dam, which they say will flood a river valley that is critical habitat for many endangered species, including jaguars living in the Cockscomb Basin Wildlife Sanctuary. "We are gambling with our natural resources, treasures that are not duplicated anywhere else in the region,"[26] said biologist Sharon Matola, director of the Belize Zoo.

But Norris Hall, a spokesman for Belize Electricity Ltd., responds that Belize needs electricity to fuel growth and development. He points out that one-third of Belizeans live in extreme poverty and need more economic opportunity: "Developing countries, such as ours, will not be able to lift themselves out of poverty without increased use of modern forms of energy,"[27] he said.

Threatened habitat: the rain forest

Nowhere is the conflict between the need for economic progress and the need to preserve natural resources more apparent than in Latin America's rain forests. In these dark, dense, tropical forests that hug the Equator, temperatures are fairly steady from 70 to 80 degrees Fahrenheit, and rainfall amounts range from 80 inches to between 200 and 300 inches every year. The constant warm temperature and ready access to water create nearly perfect conditions for life, so the rain forest is full of numerous plant and ani-

The habitat of jaguars in the Cockscomb Basin Wildlife Sanctuary could be flooded if the Belize government builds the Chalillo Dam on the Macal River.

mal species. When British naturalist Henry Walter Bates explored the Amazon River Basin and its rain forest in the 1840s, he counted some 14,712 species. In fact, although the Amazon rain forest makes up 3.5 percent of the earth's surface, it contains about 50 percent of all living species. One of these species is the jaguar, which has historically been more abundant in rain forests than in any other part of its range. The rain forest provides the jaguar with everything it needs—water, plentiful prey, and undergrowth that offers thick cover.

Yet rain forests are also a valuable natural resource for developing countries. From the stands of mahogany and cedar trees, whose woods are profitable export products, to the plentiful supply of lowland soil sought by local farmers, Latin America's rain forests are a magnet for a variety of economic pursuits. The energy of the rivers and their tributaries is harnessed for hydroelectric power, while the land is plowed up for roads and housing for expanding populations. Valuable minerals and oil have also been found in the rain forests of Latin America, resulting in major operations to extract the natural resources.

But mining and road building, and cutting and burning trees to clear the land for planting and grazing, disrupt the intricate ecosystems of the rain forest. Farming not only destroys the habitat, but rain forest soil is typically not rich in nutrients, so farmers quickly move on after a season or two, cutting further into the jungle. Chopping down trees and burning the stumps to clear for planting crops may not directly kill jaguars, but deforestation alters the natural ecosystem in ways that make the jaguar's survival more difficult. As development intrudes on the tropical forests of Mexico, Brazil, Venezuela, and other Latin American countries, the jaguar is losing the natural resources it needs to survive.

The last frontier

Rich in those natural resources are the lush grasslands and dense tropical forests surrounding the Amazon River and its tributaries. These areas are considered a critical

Sixteen million people live in the Amazon rain forest region, a critical jaguar habitat.

habitat for the jaguar and one of the few regions where the cat may be able to survive for the long term. Yet the Amazon rain forest—the world's largest surviving rain forest, sprawling outward from the banks of one of earth's most massive rivers to encompass about 2 million square miles, mostly in Brazil—is also considered to be the region's last frontier, ripe for exploitation.

After remaining intact for most of the twentieth century, beginning in the 1960s and 1970s, Brazil's interior rain forest was opened to development. A maze of new highways and airports brought hundreds of thousands of settlers into the region and eased the way for extraction of the natural resources, including large-scale mining of iron ore and bauxite, from which aluminum is made. Logging increased. Sixteen million people already live in the region, and rapid development continues, mostly unchecked.

Adding stress to the rain forest, in the mid-1990s the extreme dry weather caused by El Niño, the periodic warming of Pacific Ocean waters off the coasts of Ecuador and Peru, helped to ignite uncontrollable forest fires, which burned large sections of the forest in 1995. These burned regions will take years to renew themselves, if they are not developed in the meantime.

All this means the Amazon rain forest is being destroyed at an alarming rate, according to a 1999 study by the Global Forest Policy Project. The study estimated that 16 percent, or 217,000 square miles, of original forest has been destroyed; 17,000 square miles were lost in 1998 alone. Brazilian government estimates are lower, but no less worrisome for environmentalists. "All these estimates are quite conservative. The problem could be bigger,"[28] said ecologist Daniel C. Nepstand of the Woods Hole Research Center, one of the authors of the study.

As a result, over two hundred animals and one hundred plant species in Brazil are known to be in danger of extinction, most in the Amazon basin, including mahogany trees, the golden lion tamarin, the hyacinth macaw, and the jaguar. Even with laws protecting the rain forest from uncontrolled logging, the Brazilian government acknowledges that illegal logging and farming continue. As each acre is relinquished to development, the jaguar loses one more piece of its shrinking range.

Threats further north

The jaguar's range is shrinking not only in the Amazon but to the north as well. Mexico is considered the northern edge of the jaguar's range, but like its southerly neighbors, the country is offering less and less shelter for the big cat. Before Spanish colonization, two-thirds of Mexico was covered with forest; today, the remaining forest covers just one-fifth of the country, mostly in the south and east. The country is losing about 1.5 million acres of forest each year. For example, in the Lacandona jungle in the southern state of Chiapas, the forest shrank to 1 million acres in 1999, compared with 2.1 million acres in 1993, according to a Reuters

Two hundred animal species and one hundred plant species are in danger of extinction due to the destruction of the Amazon rain forest.

news report. Agricultural expansion and cattle ranching have pushed puma, deer, coyote, and jaguar into isolated pockets.

Elsewhere, jaguars still live in the tropical dry forest of the Chamela-Cuixmala Biosphere Reserve in central coastal

 ## Unexpected Encounter

Since jaguars were thought to have disappeared from the United States by the mid–twentieth century, the unexpected sightings of two jaguars by hunters in the remote borderlands of Mexico, Arizona, and New Mexico in 1996 made national headlines. On a ten-day hunting trip for mountain lions in March 1996, Arizona rancher Warner Glenn followed his hunting dogs up to a bluff in the Peloncillo Mountains in Arizona. There, he was startled to discover the wary eyes of a cat who had the telltale black rosette spots. "God Almighty! That's a jaguar!" Glenn exclaimed to himself, as he recounts in, *Eyes of Fire: Encounter with a Borderlands Jaguar.* "I had been 60 years waiting to see this beautiful creature." Luckily, Glenn had a camera in the saddlehorn pouch on his mule and he was able to snap a series of photographs to confirm the sighting of a jaguar.

A few months later, Jack Childs and his companions were following the trail of their barking hunting hounds up a canyon, into the rocky oak and juniper underbrush of the Baboquivari Mountains in southern Arizona. The dogs were chasing something. Childs soon discovered what it was—a full-grown jaguar. Childs photographed and videotaped the jaguar. "We all felt really blessed. I never thought I'd see a jaguar. I thought it was just something you talked about around the camp fire," said Childs in an interview with writer Peter Friederici in the June/July 1998 issue of *National Wildlife* magazine.

These two confirmed sightings of jaguars unleashed a flurry of activity in the wildlife community and raised many questions: Were jaguars living and breeding in the United States, or were these just two wanderers from Mexico? Should the United States enact laws to protect the jaguar habitat? Environmentalists, ranchers, and government policy-makers would study these issues and try to come up with answers, but for these two lucky ranchers, their encounter with a jaguar would not be forgotten. After the jaguar jumped out of sight, Glenn gathered his dogs together and headed home. Thrilled at his experience, Glenn established a jaguar fund in the Malpai Borderlands Group, an organization he belongs to that works to protect open spaces, wild lands, and the ranching economy. The funds will be used to protect the habitat of jaguars and compensate livestock owners if cattle are killed by jaguars.

Mexico, as well as in the Calakmul Biosphere Reserve, a large area of humid tropical forest in southern Mexico. But the Calakmul Biosphere Reserve, also home to tapirs, anteaters, peccaries, deer, and other prey animals, is surrounded by a growing population of subsistence farmers, which is putting pressure on the wildlife in the region, according to the World Wildlife Fund.

Ranching and jaguars

The jaguar is threatened not only by the destruction of habitat but also by the changing use of land in Latin America. Brazil's Pantanal, a sprawling grassy wetland in the interior of the country, has historically been a jaguar stronghold, but here, too, the jaguar is losing ground. In the Pantanal, in Venezuela, and in other countries, the threat comes not from logging or mining but from cattle ranching. Beginning in the sixteenth century, European settlers brought horses and cattle to Latin America, introducing an important source of income for the pioneers and new prey for the jaguar.

Unlike logging in the rain forests, cattle ranching does not destroy jaguar habitat, but it changes the use of the land in ways that pose a serious threat to the cats. The land is no longer wilderness in which the jaguar can roam freely in search of prey. Instead, millions of cattle now graze on land shared by jaguars, and the cats may attack the cattle because they are easier to catch than some wild animals. If the jaguar threatens the rancher's business by killing cattle, the cat winds up the target of the rancher's shotgun. Therefore, ranching reduces the amount of land accessible to the big cat, not unlike when a forest is leveled or a wetland is flooded.

Nuisance jaguars

Although hunting jaguars for sport and trade has been reduced by national and international laws, most countries, excluding the United States, allow people to shoot jaguars which are threatening or attacking their livestock. The hunting of problem jaguars is permitted in Brazil, Costa Rica, Guatemala, Mexico, and Peru, according to the Cat

Specialist Group of the World Conservation Union, an international group of cat experts. Other countries also allow problem jaguars to be killed. Researchers studying the jaguar diet in the Chaco region of Paraguay found that jaguars were "intensely hunted"[29] in areas with high human and cattle populations.

When Alan Rabinowitz was researching jaguars in Belize, he often found that local Indians shot jaguars they perceived as threats to their livestock, whether or not the jaguars had actually killed any of the Indians' animals. Rabinowitz and others have noted that jaguars are sometimes shot and injured, but not killed, and become further hazards to livestock, since they are too weak to return to hunting wild animals.

Since jaguars share their territory with cattle ranches in many regions, the problem of jaguars preying on cattle and being shot for their activity is serious. It is difficult for farmers to ignore a jaguar that is preying on cattle. "To poor people the loss of just a few animals represents a major financial setback, and provides a strong incentive for extermination of cat population,"[30] write Kristin Nowell and Peter Jackson. Even ranchers who are better off financially will take action to stop jaguars from attacking the source of their livelihoods.

Vanishing prey

Outside of cattle country, jaguars rely on native wild animals for food. Jaguars need to eat at least one small animal a day. But wherever jaguars are losing their habitat, they must cope as well with a dwindling supply of prey. Many of the big cat's prey are facing the same problems as the predator, from over-hunting to habitat degradation. The cat relies on the animals of the rain forests and wetlands of Central and South America, and in nearly one-third of the jaguar's range these animals are being hunted and forced from their habitats.

Among the jaguar's traditional prey are tapirs, large piglike mammals. They live east of South America's Andes Mountains in rain forests shared by the jaguar. Sought by hunters for its valuable hide, the tapir is edging toward extinction. Jaguars in Belize commonly eat anteaters, which feed on termites and insects, but anteaters are also disappearing as development intrudes on their rain forest habitat. Jaguars often comb rivers for the water-loving rodents, capybaras, which are threatened as well. Another prey of the jaguar, the Chaco tortoise of Paraguay and northern Argentina, continues to be smuggled and sold on the black market. And before a jaguar can attack it, the pampas deer of southern Brazil and northern Argentina is hunted for sport, food, and hides and is displaced by cattle ranches. As agriculture and the timber industry invade its habitat, and farmers persecute it for damaging field crops, the giant armadillo, which has served as food for the jaguar from Venezuela to northern Argentina, is declining. The Chaco peccary, also hunted by the jaguar, is similarly losing its habitat to development.

The Chaco region of Paraguay (pictured) is home to the Chaco tortoise and the Chaco peccary, two jaguar prey that are becoming scarce.

As its prey base shrinks and shifts, the jaguar must hunt farther and longer for food, adding further risks to its increasing fight for survival. When larger prey disappears, the jaguar seeks smaller prey, upsetting the ecological balance of the rain forest or grassland. Loss of prey, along with loss of habitat, is considered one of the most immediate causes of extinction of predators.

 Jaguars and Satellites

In the mountain jungles of Aengus in northeast Argentina, researchers track jaguars via satellite. A sizeable population of jaguars is believed to inhabit this jungle region bordering southern Bolivia, a nature corridor about eighty kilometers wide and two hundred kilometers long, rich with wildlife, including toucans, tapirs, monkeys, ocelots, pumas, birds, and insects. The jaguar is considered a keystone species here because it is at the top of the food chain.

The main goal of the project is to "help the local people to avoid having their cattle, sheep, and goats killed by the jaguar and . . . help the jaguar too because we would stop the local people from hunting them," said Emirian Askari of Greenpeace Argentina, one of the groups involved in the project, in a June 2000 interview with the author. Another goal is to gather information that will help convince the Argentinian government to protect the region. "The idea is to save the jungle, which is the habitat the jaguars and so many other animals need," said Askari.

The tracking project began in December 1999 when experts selected sites to set jaguar traps. The jaguars will be lured into the cages with meat. They will be given a sedative, so that the scientists can put on collars equipped with satellite transmitters and take blood samples, measurements, paw prints, and photographs. The satellite technology will be used to provide information on position and behavior. The sound transmitted from the collars will help researchers learn about the jaguar's movement, when it eats and sleeps, when it attacks prey, and when it reproduces.

Balancing act

In many ways, the jaguar, like other threatened plants and animals, is battling the clock. The United Nations predicts the population of Latin America and the Caribbean will rise from 477 million in 1995 to 809 million in the year 2050. Brazil's population grew from 54 million in 1950 to 166 million in 1998 and is expected to reach 244 million in 2050. Population growth increases the demand for fuel and electricity, and spurs the development of roads, farms and cities, all of which threaten the jaguar's range.

Where the jaguar will fit into this expanding human presence in Latin America is uncertain. Increasingly, countries realize that time is running out for saving natural places and species like the jaguar. "Preserving and maintaining suitable habitat is the biggest problem facing conservation for all cats,"[31] stated big-cat expert Maurice Hornocker. Brazilian President Fernando Enrique Cardoso recently pledged to save 10 percent of his nation's rain forests as national parks and ecologically protected areas. But the question remains whether Brazil, and the rest of Latin America, can maintain economic growth while conserving their rich, but imperiled, biodiversity.

4

Jaguars in Zoos: Ambassadors to the Wild

FEW PEOPLE WILL ever share Theodore Roosevelt's good fortune and glimpse a wild jaguar crouched in a tree in the Brazilian jungle, but zoos offer people the opportunity to safely observe the jaguar eat, sleep, or even catch a fish in a stream. Jaguars and other big cats have always been major attractions at zoos. Inviting people to actually see a live jaguar is only a small part of the modern zoo's contribution to the life of the endangered cat.

Behind the scenes, zoos work in a myriad of ways to save the jaguar and other animals that are jeopardized in the wild. Through education, scientific research, and propagation of threatened and endangered species, zoos play an important role in wildlife conservation. Zoos are helping captive jaguar populations reproduce, funding jaguar habitat conservation projects from Mexico to Venezuela, and inviting millions of people each year to learn more about the habits and habitats of the elusive big cat.

Seeing a live animal in a zoo is much more meaningful than simply reading about it. Educating both adults and children about endangered species, including the jaguar, has become an important function of zoos. The world's eleven hundred organized zoos receive at least 600 million visitors every year, according to the World Zoo Conservation Strategy, and many of those people learn a little bit more about the jaguar's threatened status, its biology and ecology, and ways to conserve the animal in the wild. The more people learn about the jaguar, the better chance the species has to survive and flourish in their natural habitats, say zoo officials. "We use these [zoo] animals as ambassadors for their cousins in the wild,"[32] said Bert Castro, living collections manager and general curator at the San Antonio Zoo.

Since jaguars are so difficult to follow in the wild, jaguars in captivity have helped scientists understand the big cat. The jaguar's DNA and reproductive behavior are of particular interest to scientists trying to learn more about sustaining the species in the long term. Zoos also help scientists learn about jaguars' behavior, nutritional needs, and the ecology they need to survive. Field biologists can test their theories on the captive animals.

Jaguar habitat in zoos

Today's zoos are a far cry from the earliest ones, which frequently consisted of traveling menageries in cages or urban parks where animals were kept behind bars in small pens with concrete floors. Only in the twentieth century did

Jaguars confined in modern zoos are often kept in environments that mimic their natural habitat.

many of America's zoos begin to create more natural habitats for their animals. In 1941, the Bronx Zoo opened its African Plains exhibit with its free-ranging, multi-species geographic habitat for African animals. Most major zoos now try to place animals, especially large mammals, in habitats that mimic their ranges in the wild. In an effort to both make the animals comfortable and educate the public about the wild habitats, zoo designers re-create entire ecosystems. Such exhibits, known as immersion exhibits, are crowd-pleasers, and the settings are also considered healthful for the animals.

Because of this trend, jaguars in zoos today are likely to live in naturalistic rain forest habitats. "Zoos are thinking more about habitat when they're building for jaguars. Typically, they try to get water features. Most zoos are expanding the space, putting in water features, climbing areas and logs for them to scratch on, and making it more naturalistic,"[33] said Robert Wiese, assistant director for animal programs at the Fort Worth Zoo, whose jaguar exhibit contains these features.

At the San Antonio Zoo, which encompasses a natural setting along the tree-lined San Antonio River and limestone cliffs, two jaguars share a 70-by-30-foot naturalistic exhibit space, with trees, rock outcroppings, a pool, and a creek. These features allow them to climb, wade in water, and hide beneath the tree foliage, as they would in the wild. The cats also have a private space, where they can spend time away from the public's view.

Some zoos have gone a step further and created exhibits that mirror both the human and ecological features of the jaguar's wild habitat. These exhibits allow people to better understand the jaguar's place in both human history and nature. For example, jaguars in the Audubon Zoo at the Audubon Institute in New Orleans are part of a larger exhibit on Mesoamerica, which focuses on both the human culture and wildlife of prehistoric Central America. The $2.2 million exhibit, which opened in 1998, invites visitors to walk a winding pathway, draped in a foggy mist, over a stream, through archways, and past replica Mayan temples and ruins to see the animal collection, which includes jabiru storks, spider monkeys, and anteaters.

Two Mexican jaguars live in the L-shaped naturalistic jaguar exhibit, which is about ninety-feet long and re-creates a Central American rain forest. With its Mayan ruins, water-fall, and stream, the space evokes the jaguar's historic home. Visitors can see the jaguars through glass in one section and through a thin wire enclosure in another, but the jaguars can retreat for privacy into a series of animal-holding areas in the Mayan temple facade.

Jaguar exhibits are popular with zoo visitors, but most jaguars pretty much ignore their human audience. Yet while one of the jaguars at the Audubon Zoo appears obliv-ious to the crowds, the other likes to track people who are watching it from behind the glass. "It's most entertaining to see children's reaction when the animal is stalking them,"[34] said Roger Iles, senior curator of mammals at the Audubon Zoo. The tracking behavior helps keep the jaguar stimulated and challenged in the zoo environment, he added.

Sometimes zoos house two jaguars together, especially if they are trying to breed them. But since the cats are solitary in the wild, they do not always get along well with each other in zoo enclosures. Some zoologists believe that ani-mals who are solitary by nature should not be placed to-gether in zoos. "When you first introduce two jaguars together, it can be a challenge to work out the social dy-namics," said Wiese. "So a lot of zoos keep them solitary."[35]

Enrichment

Whether captive jaguars are housed alone or together, zoos and wildlife centers try to keep the cats active and en-gaged in their environment, even in small enclosed spaces. Otherwise, zoo animals can become lethargic or exhibit behaviors, such as pacing, which indicate the animals are under stress.

Providing the jaguars with plenty of interesting objects to arouse their curiosity is a priority of the staff at the nonprofit Exotic Feline Breeding Compound's Feline Conservation

Center, also known as the Cat House, in Rosamond, California. At this small desert zoo north of Los Angeles, jaguars have ready access to ponds and tubs of water. They are encouraged to attack truck and car tires and chew and scratch on logs and telephone poles, just as they would pounce on prey or scratch logs in the rain forest. The staff is experimenting with scent and tactile stimulants, such as vegetables and spices, which help engage the cats with their environment and keep them alert.

Jaguars in zoos can even practice their natural predatory behavior, although in a modified way. To encourage the jaguars to become less passive during feeding time, the Audubon Zoo staff stocks the stream in the jaguar exhibit with live fish and crawfish. The jaguars are then able to stalk and catch their meal, just as they would in the wild. The jaguars also play with frozen blocks of blood residue made from the meat that they eat, which is another way for them to engage in their natural behavior. Occasionally, the staff scatters deer scents into the environment, to stimulate the jaguar's predatory instincts. "We try to change the environment to challenge them,"[36] said Iles at the Audubon Zoo.

Some zoos provide jaguars with interesting objects to arouse their curiosity.

Captive breeding

Besides their naturalistic exhibits, another way that modern zoos differ from their earlier counterparts is in the way they acquire animals. In the early days of zoos, animals were captured in the wild by animal dealers, who imported and sold them to zoos. "Animal suppliers and zoo directors burned, shot, dug and noosed their way through South American jungles, African savannas and Asian forests,"[37] writes Vicki Croke in *The Modern Ark*.

With the passages of the Endangered Species Act and the Convention on International Trade in Endangered Species in the 1970s, both of which prohibited trade in endangered species, zoos had more difficulty obtaining wild cats across international borders. Zoo exhibition was now considered a commercial use of the animal and was prohibited for endangered or threatened wild species, so zoos had to sustain their captive population through breeding programs and exchanges with other zoos.

Zoos also recognized that sustaining animal populations through captive-breeding programs would become increasingly important as more species became rare and endangered. Helping endangered animals to reproduce in zoos would allow species to avert total extinction. Endangered animals bred in zoos might eventually be reintroduced into their natural habitats to boost the wild populations.

But questions arose about captive breeding. In the 1970s, zoos began to realize that too much interbreeding among a limited population could affect the genetic diversity of future generations and even cause serious health problems for the animals. If little is known about an animal's genetic and geographical background, such as where it or its parents originally came from, then breeding produces more genetic question marks. Also, reproduction has to be controlled, because if there is a glut of one species, and no zoo wants to take the young, then the animals could wind up in inappropriate settings or even euthanized, or killed.

Species survival plans

To respond to these concerns and help maintain standards in breeding zoo animals, the American Zoo and Aquarium Association (AZA), which accredits some 184 zoos, aquariums, and wildlife centers in North America, began its Species Survival Plan program in 1981. Overseen by the AZA's Conservation and Science Department, the cooperative population management and conservation program looks at each species in all the zoos as a single population. Approximately 120 threatened and endangered animals, including the jaguar, as well as elephants and gorillas, now have Species Survival Plans, or SSPs, to ensure that they are bred in sensible and ethical ways and that their conservation in the wild is also assured. For each species, there is a separate plan, which considers which animals should be bred to increase genetic diversity in the zoo population and whether or not there are facilities willing to take the young after birth. Zoos will then loan animals to other zoos for breeding or exchange individuals in pairs that are not breeding. Every species has a stud book with the pedigree of each zoo animal, sort of a family tree with information about its parents, birth, offspring, zoos in which they live, and death.

Administered by a nine-member committee of mammal curators and jaguar experts, the Jaguar Species Survival

Two jaguars participate in a mating ritual. Zoos struggle to find ways to breed these normally solitary animals in captivity.

Plan was begun in the mid-1990s with a focus on ensuring greater variety in the genetic pool of zoo animals. At that time, little was known about the aging jaguar zoo population in the United States. Most were generic animals; that is, they were of unknown origin, born in captivity, and second-, third-, or fourth-generation zoo animals. Generally, scientists agree that generic zoo animals should not be bred, because the limited cage space should be used for purebred animals with known genetic origins.

Jaguar reproduction

The Jaguar SSP therefore recommended a voluntary moratorium, or halt, on jaguar reproduction until new jaguars, with known origins, could be introduced into the population. Meanwhile, the captive jaguar population was continuing to age and shrink. As of July 1999, there were sixty-five jaguars in about thirty AZA zoos, down from ninety-eight a few years earlier, according to the Fort Worth Zoo's Wiese, who is the coordinator of the Jaguar SSP.

The AZA is encouraging zoos to acquire directly from Latin America jaguars born in the wild or whose parents were born in the wild, so that the subspecies and geographical origin of the jaguar are known. Wild-born jaguars were acquired from Peru and Venezuela in the late 1990s. "The goal right now is to get some of the animals paired up and breeding,"[38] said Wiese. The hope is to increase the numbers of jaguars to about 120, but that will take time.

Yet zoos have to be careful how many jaguars reproduce since there has to be a place for every young jaguar to go after it is born. Most zoos with breeding jaguars do not have the space for the cubs to grow up in. "What you produce, you have to place. Every zoo would love to have newborn jaguars," said Iles at the Audubon Zoo. "A lot of zoos are interested in displaying jaguars but you have to be careful how many you reproduce. You have to make good decisions."[39]

Breeding takes time and patience

While jaguars have successfully reproduced in zoos, sometimes it is difficult to breed these normally solitary animals in

The Jaguar's Chaco

Researchers with the San Diego Zoo's Center for Reproduction of Endangered Species journeyed to the remote Chaco region of Paraguay to help find ways to preserve this unique habitat, one of the jaguar's few remaining strongholds. The Chaco region, which reaches into Bolivia, Argentina, and Brazil, is a palm and scrub forest, with dense thorny scrub. Parts of it are protected in parks and sanctuaries, but even these areas are vulnerable to human activity.

For most of history, this inaccessible area, with its plethora of wildlife, was left untouched. But the Trans-Chaco Highway recently opened the Chaco to wood gatherers, hunters, ranchers, and developers. Mennonites have cattle ranches here, and indigenous people cut and gather wood. Because they are living perilously close to humans, jaguars are frequently shot by ranchers and poachers. The San Diego Zoo is one of many conservation organizations trying to find a balance in the Chaco between economic growth and habitat preservation. The zoo is seeking to educate and enlist the help of local residents to protect and enlarge the Chaco's parks and sanctuaries and shield the region's rich biodiversity.

captivity. Finding a pair that will produce offspring is not always easy. "We've got a number of pairs set up to breed, but they are not conceiving. Right now we have a lot of older jaguars and not too many are breeding," said Wiese in the spring of 2000. A jaguar in her late teens at the Wildlife World Zoo in Litchfield Park, Arizona, is among the few zoo jaguars that have produced cubs in recent years—she and her mate have had nineteen cubs in ten litters. Scientists have found that jaguars that are too familiar with each other may not mate. To encourage successful breeding, zoos may try to change aspects of the environment or enrich and change the jaguar's diet. But there may be many reasons for a jaguar failing to conceive, and Wiese acknowledges that there is still a lot to learn about captive breeding of jaguars. "We're hoping to figure it out,"[40] said Wiese.

In the spring of 2000, San Antonio Zoo workers were carefully monitoring Dominique, a twelve-year-old female jaguar, and Piedras, a fifteen-year-old male jaguar on loan from the Houston Zoo for the purpose of breeding. The match between the two jaguars was recommended by the AZA's SSP jaguar committee. Unlike some jaguar pairs, which cannot live peaceably with each other, the cats seemed to get along well. They received a typical large-carnivore diet of horse meat, along with vitamins. They seemed to tolerate the many zoo visitors but mainly ignored them. Still, Dominique did not become pregnant that spring. The zoo made plans to test the animals to see if there were any physical reasons for the apparent infertility.

The Audubon Zoo imported two jaguars from Mexico in the late 1990s to introduce a new genetic pool into the jaguar population in the United States. After two years, the two young jaguars had yet to conceive, but zoo officials were still optimistic. Many factors contribute to successful conception, such as compatibility, space, and the age of the

Captive breeding opponents claim that jaguars born in the programs will expand the zoo population, but will not help the survival of the species.

jaguars. If the two jaguars do not breed successfully, the staff at the Audubon Zoo may eventually test the viability of the male's sperm. If it is viable, the zoo could implant it in the female. If the sperm count is low, the zoo can rotate the male to another zoo and bring in a new male to try again.

New trends and controversy

One promising area of research to increase successful breeding of jaguars is the use of assisted reproduction techniques. In coming years, *in vitro* fertilization, artificial insemination, and embryo transfer may be used to expand the captive jaguar population and increase its genetic diversity. Yet zoo curators are moving cautiously, since these techniques are expensive and may not be necessary. At the Audubon Zoo, zoo officials want to wait as long as possible before stepping in. "Our goal is to allow them to breed naturally,"[41] said Iles.

Nevertheless, captive-breeding programs can be controversial. Some people say that all the zoos are doing is expanding the zoo population, not helping the survival of the species. Defenders of Wildlife, a Washington, D.C.-based conservation group, is concerned that unless animals can be returned to the wild safely, captive breeding only creates zoo specimens. The United Kingdom-based Cat Survival Trust, a private organization that supports wild-cat conservation, originally planned to breed jaguars and other cats in captivity and release them to the wild, but then decided the most important priority should be preserving the remaining habitat for the animals. Recently, the trust purchased land in Argentina to protect wild cats.

Reintroducing captive animals in the wild

However controversial, captive breeding becomes increasingly important for endangered animals if the species should become extinct in the wild or disappear from part of its range. In 1907, the Bronx Zoo used its zoo population of American bison to restock four reserves in the West. American bison had been hunted to near extinction and would have been lost forever without the zoo animals to re-

vive the wild populations. Since then, other endangered animals, including the black-footed ferret, the golden lion tamarind, and the Arabian oryx, have been bred in zoos and successfully reintroduced to the wild, giving new hope to the species. Also, captive animals may offer a source of new genetic material to infuse diversity into depleted wild populations.

Despite these successes with other species, reintroducing captive jaguars into the wild is not considered a practical way to stabilize or increase the species. Jaguars have disappeared from their range because of human persecution, habitat loss, and the depletion of their prey. Unless these threats are diminished, it is unlikely jaguars will thrive in the wild. "In the case of the jaguar, the northern and southern parts of its former range are now heavily settled, and hardly present ideal conditions for reintroduction,"[42] write Kristin Nowell and Peter Jackson.

Reintroducing jaguars into the wild could pose a risk to the cat, as well as to its prey animal population and even to humans in the region. Jaguars bred in captivity are unused

Reintroducing captive jaguars into the wild is not considered a practical way to restore the species.

to surviving and hunting in the wilderness. Zoo animals are not sufficiently afraid of people and so could come perilously close to humans, risking being shot or even posing a threat. In addition, the prey animals in the area may not be used to eluding jaguars and could become depleted too rapidly, upsetting the local ecological balance.

Scientists would also prefer to return jaguars to the areas from which their particular subspecies originated. Since the current stock of captive jaguars is mostly of unknown origin, it would be difficult to place individual jaguars in their correct ancestral homes. In the future, as zoos begin to breed jaguars from known origins, this may be more of a possibility.

Because of all these problems, scientists are not eager to risk the lives of individual jaguars by placing them in the wild. The jaguar population has not reached the critical point of the snow leopard or tiger, which have diminished to the point of near extinction. So for now, scientists are concentrating on saving the habitat that remains for the jaguar. "If we can raise funds for parks in Central and South America," said Wiese, "we can create places for jaguars to live so we won't get to the state that tigers are in and other really endangered animals."[43]

Zoo research in the field

As Wiese points out, zoos' efforts to serve as refuges for animals that are endangered, or even extinct, in the wild, can have only a limited effect if there is no wild habitat left for the animals to survive in or return to. Therefore, zoo organizations, such as the Wildlife Conservation Society (WCS), are increasingly concentrating on saving wild habitat. "WCS knows that if zoos are serious about saving species, they must actively save wild places,"[44] writes Vicki Croke.

Conservation has been a goal of AZA zoos since the early 1980s and is even more so today. "We are now focusing on habitat conservation. Zoos used to focus on species, but if there's not enough habitat for them, then it's really futile," said Castro at the San Antonio Zoo. "Our focus is to educate people about habitat conservation and trying to save and salvage some of the areas jaguars have lived in."[45] The AZA has started requiring that zoos directly engage in wildlife conservation to help stem the destruction of natural habitat around the world. According to the AZA, there are about seven hundred zoo-sponsored conservation projects in eighty countries. Nearly half the AZA zoos and aquariums sponsor conservation projects in the field.

The WCS, long a leader among American zoos in wildlife conservation, helped fund the creation of the world's only jaguar reserve in Belize in the 1980s. In 1999, the WCS launched a five-year program to save the jaguar, its most major effort so far on behalf of the big cat.

Private feline organizations

In contrast with zoos, which have to be concerned about all their species, private organizations dedicated to nondomestic cats provide public education and, in some cases, fund research projects exclusively on the jaguar and its cousins in the wild. Often begun by people with a passion for wild cats, these organizations fill a need for education and outreach, particularly in the United States, where people do not have much contact with wild cats. These small facilities, some of which work closely with the AZA, are supported mostly by donations and memberships. And they are good sources of information on captive behavior, reproduction, and conservation of wild cats.

Some jaguars are studied by private feline organizations, which are committed to the preservation of nondomestic cats.

One of these organizations, the Sierra Endangered Cat Haven, a for-profit educational organization in the foothills of the Sierra Nevada Mountains in Dunlap, California, houses eighteen different cat species in its desert facility, which is open to the public. Meanwhile, its sister organization, Project Survival, a nonprofit education and conservation organization

for wild cats, is sponsoring the "Protect the Jaguar" endowment fund to support jaguar research projects in the field. "Protect the Jaguar" is assisting biologists in Paraguay who are conducting the first general cat survey in the dry Gran Chaco region of northern Paraguay and southern Bolivia. Jaguars are thought to be plentiful in this arid forest, and researchers are using camera traps along trails to count the cats.

Project Survival is also working with a Brazilian biologist who is developing new reproductive techniques that may eventually allow wild cats to be impregnated with the embryos of captive jaguars. "All of the artificial insemination techniques aren't consistent or reliable yet,"[46] said Project Survival's president Dale Anderson. But, he predicts that frozen semen from wild jaguars may become one resource to help keep the species alive.

Zoos in the wild

Zoos have come a long way in the past fifty years, and the changes in them are promising for the jaguar. While zoos gradually create more naturalistic homes for jaguars in captivity, they are also putting more money and effort into saving the jaguar by selective breeding of captive animals and conservation research in the field. Although they are still focused on drawing visitors to their zoological parks, they are trying to aid in the survival of wild animal species. "You have to, as an institution, be committed to doing what's best for the species, not just for your institution,"[47] said Iles at the Audubon Zoo.

5

Saving the Jaguar

PROTECTING A LARGE carnivore like the jaguar is an enormous task, one that demands a complex safety network of environmental laws, reserves and parks, public policy, and education. As jaguars increasingly share their territory with people, the challenge becomes greater. The big cat's future is even more precarious than the future of some threatened species because people may perceive the jaguar, like other predators and all big cats, as a danger to life and property.

Critical pieces of the jaguar's safety net have already begun to be put in place, including wildlife protection laws, protected habitat in parks and reserves, outreach to cattle ranchers who live in jaguar territory, and new research into the life and habits of the jaguar. But jaguar experts agree the solitary and elusive cat will survive the twenty-first century only with extraordinary efforts and the cooperation of many people, from zoologists to politicians, from international conservationists to local citizens who share the jaguar's land.

Jaguar preserve

A good example of the benefits of cooperation culminated in 1986 when Belize took the bold step of setting aside land for the world's first, and only, jaguar preserve. This victory for the jaguar came about through the efforts of one man, with the support of wildlife organizations, the Belize government, and an international car company.

In 1983, Alan Rabinowitz, a wildlife ecologist with what is now the Wildlife Conservation Society (WCS), traveled to the remote Cockscomb Basin, a mountainous rain forest in Belize, to study the jaguar in its natural habitat and figure out how to reduce conflicts between jaguars and livestock. At the time, the jaguar was one of the least understood of the big cats. The only formal study of jaguars in the wild had been conducted by two scientists in Brazil in the 1970s.

Jaguars were still considered nuisances by Belizeans. Not until 1982 had the Belizean government banned the hunting of jaguars, though farmers could still shoot jaguars who had killed cattle. The local Mayan Indians had long ago lost their ancestors' sense of awe toward the jaguar. Instead, they considered the jaguar a threat to their livestock and often shot the animal on sight. Rabinowitz confirmed at least ten jaguars killed in a four-year period by timber workers and Indians in Cockscomb.

With much perseverance, Rabinowitz managed to win the Indians' trust and enlist some of them to help track jaguars through the rugged jungle. He was able to capture a few jaguars in makeshift cages and sedate them long enough to attach radio collars before releasing them. Then he tracked the cats, collecting valuable information on their diet, sleep, behavior, and territories. Rabinowitz also helped change the attitudes of some of the Indians from wanting to kill jaguars to wanting to save them.

Then in 1986, due to Rabinowitz's efforts to convince Belize that the jaguar needed protection, the country declared the Cockscomb Basin Wildlife Sanctuary, a region formerly logged for mahogany, a jaguar preserve. Jaguars could no longer be shot there, nor could the forest be logged. Park buildings were constructed to bring tourists to the area as a source of revenue. Wildlife Conservation International, now WCS, Jaguar Cars of Canada, and the WWF helped to fund the preserve, and the Belize Audubon Society managed the sanctuary, which was expanded in 1990.

After his work in Belize was finished, Rabinowitz went on to study tigers in Thailand and leopards in Borneo and Taiwan, yet he worried about the jaguar. He later wrote,

"Though remnants of the spirit of both the jaguar and the old Maya still survive in isolated pockets, how long can they last? In half a century, will the only live jaguars be in zoos?"[48]

A jaguar from the Cockscomb Basin Wildlife Sanctuary, declared a jaguar preserve in 1986.

Protecting the jaguar from the fur trade

As Rabinowitz recognized, the Cockscomb sanctuary protects only a limited population of jaguars in Belize. In contrast, laws shielding the jaguar from the fur trade and prohibiting sport hunting have had a broader impact. The jaguar survived the twentieth century, in large part, because many nations decided to protect endangered species from indiscriminate killing by traders and hunters.

International trade laws, principally the Convention on International Trade in Endangered Species, or CITES, restricted and regulated trade in wildlife. All Latin American countries with jaguar populations are now members of CITES, as is the United States. Trade in the jaguar dramatically dropped, and by the 1990s, the number of jaguars, dead or alive, traded internationally was negligible by most accounts. Today, clothing or rugs that appear to be made from jaguar fur are more likely to be faux, or fake. In fact, "faux jaguar" is a popular pattern for rugs, clothing, wallpaper, and other decorative items. The fur used in today's fur products does not come from endangered wild animals, like the jaguar, a practice that is now both politically unpopular and illegal.

Protecting endangered species

National laws protecting endangered species also helped stabilize the jaguar population. Spurred by the environmental movement, many nations passed wildlife protection laws in the 1970s and 1980s. The jaguar was originally listed as an endangered species in the United States in the Endangered Species Conservation Act of 1969. This act, which offered protection to plants and animals, kept two separate lists of wildlife: one for foreign species and one for species native to the United States. Because there had been few sightings of the jaguar in the United States, the cat was listed only as an endangered foreign wildlife.

Congress passed the Endangered Species Act (ESA) in 1973, and the foreign and native lists were replaced by a single list of endangered and threatened wildlife. But through a series of oversights, the jaguar and six other endangered species were left off the list, even though the U.S. Fish and Wildlife Service, which administers the law, acknowledged that the big cat should be federally protected. It was not until 1997, after two jaguars were sighted in the United States near the Mexican border, that the jaguar was listed as an endangered species.

With ESA listing, the jaguar is protected from being hunted, shot, trapped, traded, or sold. A person cannot even sell an old jaguar coat that has been hanging in the closet for years. Killing an endangered species is a federal crime, and violators face significant fines and/or imprisonment. In addition, some states, including New Mexico and California, have their own laws protecting jaguars and prohibiting people from importing, transporting, possessing, or selling jaguars without special permits relating to research or zoos.

In the 1970s and 1980s, Latin American countries also established environmental agencies and passed laws to protect their endangered plants and animals. Today, most countries with jaguar populations have laws that prohibit, or at least regulate, the killing of jaguars. In Costa Rica, for example, conservation laws prohibit the jaguar from being hunted and killed. Sport hunting, once a popular recreation in countries with jaguars, has diminished because of protective laws for endangered species. Belize, for example, outlawed sport hunting of the jaguar in the early 1980s.

Yet while the United States, for the most part, has the funds and staff to implement its environmental laws, many countries with jaguars lack the resources to enforce their

In the 1970s greater awareness of the potential for jaguar extinction began to take hold.

The Jaguar Conservation Team

When it comes to the Endangered Species Act, ranchers and environmentalists often vehemently disagree. To comply with the protective standards of the law, ranchers sometimes have to give up their rights to use their land as they please, if it has been identified as critical habitat for an endangered plant or animal. At the same time, environmentalists complain the ranchers, by protesting for their land rights, are blocking efforts to save vanishing wildlife. But after two jaguars were sighted in Arizona in 1996, the two communities found a way to reach common ground.

In 1997, the Jaguar Conservation Team was established to protect and learn more about the jaguars in the Southwest. Federal officials, environmentalists, ranchers, and others with an interest in the jaguar joined the group. Despite their usually clashing views on environmental issues, they recognized the jaguar is part of the natural history of the region and should be protected. Even ranchers were willing to find ways to live with the jaguar. "One thing is for sure, it will take all of our efforts to protect this animal and the wide open country it needs," commented Warner Glenn, the second-generation Arizona rancher and mountain lion hunting guide, in *Eyes of Fire: Encounter with a Borderlands Jaguar*, his book about sighting a jaguar in 1996.

For the jaguar to thrive in the borderlands, it will need protection from being hunted, adequate prey, and movement corridors to connect it with the jaguar populations in Mexico. The conservation team is concentrating on saving the jaguar's habitat in Mexico, since it is the Mexican jaguar population that has probably been wandering into the United States for hundreds of years. "The key to jaguar conservation in the United States is conservation of the species in Mexico," said Bill Van Pelt, a member of the Jaguar Conservation Team, in an interview. "We'd like to still be able to provide jaguars the opportunity to exist as they have for hundreds of years."

endangered species laws and manage protected wild areas. Although laws shielding the jaguar from poaching and hunting in most countries have helped save the cat, it is still being shot and killed in one-third of its range, according to a WCS report. Advocates for the jaguar would like to see better enforcement of existing wildlife protection laws.

Managing predators near people and livestock

At the same time, jaguar experts are searching for innovative solutions to reduce conflicts between people and jaguars, since the majority of jaguars share their habitat to some extent with humans. Finding ways to minimize the real or perceived threat of jaguars to cattle ranchers and others who live in the big cat's territory will go a long way toward protecting the species, say jaguar experts.

In 1998, to reduce the problem of jaguars killing live-stock, scientists and ranchers tested different types of fencing at Hato Pinero, a ranch in Venezuela, to keep jaguars away from calves. Researchers there hoped to find ways to discourage cats from killing cattle so that the ranchers will tolerate jaguars on their land rather than shoot them.

Another option to reduce jaguar problems for cattle ranchers is to move individual jaguars away from the area. Translocation of problem jaguars has been tried in Belize and other countries, with inconclusive results. Often jaguars that are relocated continue to kill livestock. But scientists are still studying the possibility of moving problem jaguars to different locations, to keep them from being killed.

Since it has both the largest population of jaguars in Latin America and a major cattle industry, Brazil is confronting this problem directly. The Brazilian government, with support from the World Conservation Union (IUCN), established the National Centre for Research, Management and Conservation of Predators in the late 1990s to solve livestock-predator problems. The center is undertaking field studies, and trying to relocate problem jaguars away from cattle ranches. Education programs are being offered to ranchers to help them find ways to keep their cattle safe. The center may experiment with compensating ranchers for cattle loss to avert jaguar killing.

Jaguar experts also are tackling the problem of the indiscriminate killing of jaguars that are not attacking livestock. Sometimes jaguars are shot for no apparent reason, except that they have encountered humans. For example, researchers for the WCS found that of the thirty-nine jaguars killed in two reserves in the Brazilian Amazon from 1994 to 1999, only about half were killed for reportedly attacking the subsistence fishermen and farmers in the area, or their livestock. The researchers could not find an explanation for the other jaguar deaths. "Jaguars were either shot from trees or in the water or harpooned and killed in the water,"[49] write Cheryl Chetkiewicz and Gleb Raygorodetsky.

These researchers, and other jaguar experts, agree that, along with enforcing and strengthening wildlife protection laws, scientists must educate people about jaguar behavior and livestock safety in order to reduce jaguar killings.

Saving jaguar habitat

Jaguar advocates are also trying to find ways to preserve the big cat's habitat, which like all wild land is vulnerable to development and changing uses. The World Resources Institute, an environmental research organization, predicts the single greatest cause of species extinction in the next fifty years will be tropical deforestation. Since jaguars are scattered widely in many countries, each with its own environmental policies, protecting the cat's wild land, much of which is in the tropics, is not simple.

There are, however, signs of progress. Many Latin American countries have tried to slow the destruction of wild areas, including jaguar habitat, by creating national parks and reserves. The amount of land protected in reserves varies from country to country, as does the management of parks and reserves. While Belize protects nearly half of its land, other countries have permitted more pri-

Efforts to save jaguar habitat include the establishment of national parks and reserves.

vate ownership and development. "In most places, a system of protected areas have provided core refuges for jaguars, but the quality, infrastructure, and support varies,"[50] said Chetkiewicz, program officer for the WCS's Jaguar Conservation Program, begun in 1999.

Hundreds of tourists travel to Cockscomb Basin Wildlife Sanctuary every year hoping to see the preserve's jaguars.

Environmentalists recognize that conservation efforts succeed in the long run only when local residents participate in and even profit from them. By protecting their natural resources, some countries have reaped direct economic benefits. For example, 40 percent of Belize is protected in parks and reserves, and ecotourism, or the industry of attracting tourists to see Belize's monkeys, manatees, scarlet macaws, and jaguars, is a significant part of the national economy. The Cockscomb Basin Wildlife Sanctuary attracts hundreds of tourists with an interest in jaguars to Belize every year.

Costa Rica has been another pioneer in protecting its natural resources. Today, some 25 percent of the country, which has a coast on both the Caribbean Sea and the Pacific Ocean, is protected in national parks, forest reserves, and Indian reservations. Like Belize, Costa Rica has found ecotourism to be highly profitable. Nature enthusiasts from around the world travel to see Costa Rica's butterflies, birds such as the quetzal and the toucan, fourteen hundred tree species, and monkeys, sloths, tapirs, armadillos, and jaguars. This industry brings funds into the country and gives local residents a tangible incentive to protect their wildlife.

Saving a forest, saving jaguars

With their ability to bridge national borders, international environmental organizations have led the way in identifying and trying to protect regions and species in Latin America that are vulnerable. The World Wide Fund

 The Cat Specialist Group

The best place to go for scientific facts and practical knowledge about wild cats and their conservation is the Cat Specialist Group of the IUCN's Species Survival Commission. Some 160 field biologists, wildlife managers, government officials, and specialists from fields like genetics, environmental law, and wildlife traffic, representing fifty countries, volunteer their time and knowledge for wild cat conservation. The group advises the Convention on International Trade in Endangered Species, the World Conservation Monitoring Centre, and any organizations that seek assistance on cats. It also publishes a newsletter, *Cat News*, with the latest field research on wild cats, and consolidates and disseminates information on wild cats.

In 1996, the group published *Wild Cats: Status Survey and Conservation Action Plan*, a look at the wild cats of the world and what must be done to save them. Although the jaguar is not as threatened as the tiger, snow leopard, Iberian lynx, and Andean mountain cat, the Cat Specialist Group ranks the jaguar as actively threatened, with high levels of hunting pressure.

for Nature with its staff of scientists and conservationists, is working with governments and conservationists in Latin America to save endangered ecosystems and preserve biodiversity. One of the WWF's two hundred conservation projects in the region is protecting the Misiones Forest, where jaguars may have a chance to survive.

The Atlantic Forest of Brazil once painted a sweeping green swath down the country's east coast and into parts of Paraguay and Argentina, spanning some 478,764 square miles and teeming with plant and animal life. But in the five hundred years since Brazil was colonized, much of the wilderness was clear-cut for farms and cattle, and Brazil's sprawling cities of São Paulo and Rio de Janeiro are located there. Today, only about 5 percent of the Atlantic Forest remains undisturbed. Because of this loss of wild space, scientists surmise that jaguars have essentially been lost from coastal Brazil.

However, the Misiones Forest, a surviving interior fragment of the original Atlantic Forest that is shared by Argentina, Paraguay, and Brazil, still may offer some protection for the jaguar. The WWF and other groups are trying to help the three countries develop a management scheme to protect it from further degradation, for here is one place that the jaguar, and its prey, may be able to survive for the long term.

Biosphere reserves

Another international effort to save the fragile habitat of jaguars and other wildlife is UNESCO's Man and the Biosphere Program. This program, which includes 369 biosphere reserves in ninety-one countries, attempts to balance conservation of ecosystems and biodiversity with economic and social development and cultural preservation. Usually, the biosphere reserves offer a further layer of protection to areas already within national parks and conservation areas.

Many of the biosphere reserves in Latin America contain jaguar habitat. The Maya Biosphere Reserve, located

The jaguar and many of its prey, including the coati (pictured), are protected in biosphere reserves.

in southern Mexico, northern Guatemala, and Belize, is one of them. With rivers, lakes, swamps, and flooding savannas, as well as ancient ruins of the Mayan culture, this large tropical rain forest is home to the jaguar and many of its prey animals, including the armadillo, hooded skunk, and long-tailed weasel. Many of these animals, like the jaguar, are threatened species.

With scientists conducting research and environmental education, and encouraging local residents to participate in managing the area, the jaguar and its prey are safer in the Maya Biosphere Reserve than in most places. However, a major environmental concern when it comes to protected areas is what lies outside their borders. Surrounding the Maya Reserve is a buffer area, where local people work to support themselves by cattle grazing, hunting, fishing; farming beans, maize, and other vegetables; and harvesting forest resources. While some of the activities do threaten the jaguar, the buffer area allows people to engage in work without inflicting much harm, and thus reduces the level of resentment toward jaguars and other wildlife.

Yet, in the Maya Biosphere Reserve and other protected areas, conservationists continue to remain vigilant to preserve the precarious balance of nature. Protected areas need to be managed, both inside and outside their borders. Despite designations as parks or reserves, many areas remain vulnerable to intrusions such as logging and wildlife poaching. According to one report, some forty jaguars were killed during three years in the late 1990s in the Iguacu National Park in Brazil, a biosphere reserve. The Manu National Park in Peru, the Calamus Biosphere Reserve in Southern Mexico, and the Chico forests in Ecuador and Colombia all report the presence of jaguars, but each is threatened by development, illegal logging, and farming, according to wildlife experts.

Wildlife corridors

Since jaguars can roam hundreds of miles, any effort to save the big cat's habitat has to recognize that the jaguar will wander outside the borders of parks and reserves. Wildlife corridors, or safe passageways, where animals can move freely to feed, mate, and roam between protected areas, are essential for the cat's survival. Jaguar experts are trying to identify wildlife corridors in the Amazon, Belize, and other regions that link jaguar feeding grounds and safe habitats.

For example, a small population of jaguars has been identified approximately 130 miles south of the U.S. border in the Mexican state of Sonora. This is probably the population from which individuals have occasionally wandered up into the southwestern United States. The region connecting Sonora and the United States, though still undeveloped, is threatened with mining, roads, and other development, and jaguar advocates would like to protect it for use by the roaming jaguars. "A lot of people don't realize they may need huge areas to live in, but they still need narrow strips of habitat for movement. Typically planners neglect to identify movement corridors,"[51] said Bill Van Pelt, non-game mammals program manager for the Arizona Fish and Wildlife Department and a member of the Jaguar Conservation Team, a group trying to protect jaguars.

Saving the jaguar's Amazon

Protecting the Amazon rain forest is a priority for jaguar researchers and other conservationists, who recognize that the loss of a rain forest not only wipes out individual species, but contributes to water pollution, soil erosion, and other serious environmental problems. Because of its rich biodiversity and vast size, the Amazon has the potential for harboring the jaguar for a long time to come. "Amazonia has been described as a critically important area for the jaguar, and is generally believed to be the best

 Cars and Cats

In 1935, British automobile mogul William Lyons was looking for a unique name to help create a new, sleek, powerful image for his cars. Lyons' advertising agency supplied him with a list of animal names. Jaguar, the swift jungle cat with an exotic moniker, appealed to Lyons, but to use the name, he had to obtain permission from Armstrong-Siddeley Ltd., which had already named an airplane engine after the wild cat. The new Jaguar automobile line for 1936 featured the company's first real sports car, the S.S. Jaguar 100. Eventually, the company became Jaguar Cars Ltd., and the cars, Jaguars.

The company that is so identified with the wild cat has in recent years taken steps to save it. When the government of Belize decided to protect the Cockscomb Basin Wildlife Sanctuary for jaguars in 1986, Jaguar Cars of Canada donated money to fix and build park buildings for workers and tourists. In 1999, Jaguar Cars North America pledged $1 million over a five-year period for jaguar conservation research at the Wildlife Conservation Society. "Most people usually aren't able to donate the kind of money that's needed to save an entire species of animal," said Terry Nelson, Jaguar dealer marketing manager, on the WCS website. "That's why corporate sponsorship of conservation is critical and why we're very happy to be involved in helping this beautiful animal."

area for the long-term survival of jaguar populations,"[52] states the WCS on its website.

But slowing down the deforestation, mining, colonization, and building of hydroelectric dams that have intruded on Amazonia since the 1960s is a huge challenge, since Brazil and other countries in the region have serious economic stakes in the rain forest. Protecting the land often interferes with activities to improve the lives of the people, such as building roads and starting up businesses.

As early as 1978, the eight nations sharing the Amazon rain forest signed the Amazonia Treaty to manage protected areas in the region. But development continued mostly unabated. Faced with growing international pressure to take action, in the late 1990s, Brazil stiffened its laws protecting the rain forest and stepped up enforcement measures to stop illegal logging, mining, pollution,

Efforts to hinder the destruction of the Amazon rain forest (pictured) often interfere with construction that improves the lives of people living in the region.

and poaching. To stem deforestation, Brazilian president Fernando Enrique Cardoso in 1999 sent out armed forces to block illegal logging in the Amazon Basin. The following year, the Brazilian government announced increased funding for patrols to watch for illegal logging and fires, set by peasants to clear the jungle for livestock grazing and crops. To better monitor activity in remote areas of the Amazon, Brazil is spending over $1 billion to develop a system to monitor the Amazon with satellites, aircraft, and radar.

Although jaguar experts believe that the Amazon is the heart and core of the jaguar's range, as recently as 2000, no scientific studies had been done to count the jaguars in the Amazon. Little information is even available on the occurrence of jaguars in the southern Amazon Basin. As the rain forest becomes ever more vulnerable, scientists recognize the urgency of finding out where jaguars are in the region, and how many, in order to add their voices to the call to save the Amazon.

Hope for the jaguar in the new millennium

To better understand and protect the jaguar population in the Amazon and other regions, in 1999, the world's top jaguar researchers met in Mexico City for a conference, "Jaguars in the New Millenium," organized by the WCS and the Universidad Nacional Autonoma de Mexico. For the first time, jaguar researchers, scattered in many countries and studying different aspects of the wild cat, were able to share information and discuss conservation strategies.

Scientists at the conference reported where they had seen jaguars or evidence of jaguars. The WCS staff then took the data and compiled a Geographic Information System map of the animal, highlighting its known range. "There have been some reviews of jaguar ecology and conservation in the past, but none of them has been as geographically explicit as this one,"[53] said WCS Associate Conservation Ecologist Eric Anderson. This data is critical so that scientists can plan the best strategies to save the big cats.

Researchers are using this information to determine where jaguars have the best chance for long-term survival and how to protect those regions. "We were able to start prioritizing which places look like the best jaguar areas from our current knowledge and places where we have to find out more information,"[54] said Alan Rabinowitz, who spearheaded the conference. The conference set in motion another effort in the WCS's long history of trying to save the world's large carnivores, the Jaguar Conservation Program, led by Rabinowitz and a team of jaguar experts. The WCS hopes to assist jaguars before they become highly endangered. "With proper intervention, there is still time to save these magnificent predators in areas where their numbers are strong. Despite all odds, it's a battle than can be won,"[55] stated the WCS in an ad on the Op-Ed page of the *New York Times* announcing the program.

The jaguar program, at a cost of $4 million for the first five years, is developing jaguar conservation solutions tailored to particular regions and in concert with local government and conservation groups. Separate research projects are underway in the Brazilian Pantanal, the Cockscomb Basin of Belize, and other areas to find out more about jaguar behavior and ecological requirements in different habitats. "The threats to jaguars are consistent—opportunistic hunting, loss of prey, and habitat destruction—but the solutions might be specific to the country and the landscape,"[56] said program officer Chetkiewicz. For example, the WCS plans to work with ranchers in the Pantanal to find ways to avert conflicts between jaguars and cattle.

Developing standards for researching the jaguar is another WCS priority. Scientists need to know more about jaguar genetics and health and to develop standardized methods for gathering this information. A WCS researcher in northern Belize is testing the effectiveness of using camera traps, analyzing jaguar tracks and droppings, and using radio collars to see which technology works best in certain habitats.

Scientists now have the technology to learn more about the jaguar in order to save it.

The WCS is also supporting long-term ecological studies in the field, including a study on the ecology and conservation of white-lipped peccaries and jaguars in Costa Rica's Corcovado National Park. Peccaries, also an endangered species, are a food source for local people and for the jaguars. Thirty peccaries and four jaguars are being followed using radio collars so that scientists can estimate survival, reproduction, home ranges, movement, and activity. This information will enable scientists to see whether available food can sustain both species.

Glory departed

Curiosity about the elusive jaguar is nothing new, but now scientists have the tools and a strong motivation—the jaguar's threatened status—to learn more about the cat in order to save it. Decades ago, the pioneering conservationist Aldo Leopold often explored the delta of the Colorado, the swampy wetland, once home to the jaguar, where the Colorado River empties into the Gulf of Mexico. Leopold hoped to see the animal, which he called "the despot of the Delta, the great jaguar, *el tigre*." But as early as the 1920s, Leopold could find no sign of the big cat. As Leopold wrote in his environmental classic, *A Sand County Almanac*, "We saw neither hide nor hair of him, but his personality pervaded the wilderness; no living beast forgot his potential presence, for the price of unwariness was death. . . . Freedom from fear has arrived, but a glory has departed from the green lagoons."[57]

As the search for the jaguar goes farther into the heart of its range, people concerned about the species recognize that it will take extraordinary efforts for the jaguar to survive. As more is learned about the jaguar and its precarious status, attitudes toward the jaguar are changing. Mayan Indian Ernesto Saqui was the manager of the Cockscomb Basin Wildlife Sanctuary when a *Boston Globe* reporter stopped by in 1989. Saqui told the reporter that he had been killing jaguars to sell to American smugglers since he was a teenager, making more money from the pelt of a single jaguar than his family made all year as farmers. But, he said, he no longer would think of hurting the big cat; he now believes, as his ancient Mayan ancestors once did, that the jaguar is both sacred and courageous. "It makes me cry when I see a dead jaguar now,"[58] he said.

Saqui is one of many people who have helped give the jaguar the possibility of a long-term future. While the status of the jaguar is grim in some places, with small isolated populations fending off poachers and habitat conversion, elsewhere the big cat may have a good chance of survival. "Unlike the tiger, the jaguar still occupies some habitats with vast relatively uninterrupted tracts of land, where threats are relatively low and the long term probability of survival is high,"[59] wrote WCS scientists in a paper on findings from the millennium conference. Finding ways for people and jaguars to share the rain forests and grasslands of Latin America will be a challenge, and advocates for the jaguar are working hard to find solutions. "Fortunately, we're not at the stage that they're highly endangered," said Robert Wiese, coordinator of the Jaguar Species Survival Plan. "If we do our job, they'll never get to that place."[60]

Notes

Introduction

1. Belize National Parks, Natural Reserves and Wildlife Sanctuaries. http://ambergriscaye.com/pages/town/park cockscomb.html.

2. Lily Whiteman, "Violence, Lies and Videotape," *E/The Environmental Magazine,* May/June 1997. www.emagazine. com/may-june_1997/0597curr_3.html.

Chapter 1: The Jaguar and Its Behavior

3. Richard Perry, *The World of the Jaguar.* New York: Taplinger Publishing, 1970, p. 22.

4. Theodore Roosevelt, *Through the Brazilian Wilderness.* New York: Charles Scribner's Sons, 1914, p. 79.

5. Quoted in David Arnold, "In Belize, a Hunter Turns Protector," *Boston Globe*, March 20, 1989, p. 2.

6. Quoted in Don E. Wilson and Sue Ruff, eds, *The Smithsonian Book of North American Mammals.* Washington, DC and London: Smithsonian Institute Press, 1999, p. 236.

7. Dan Koeppel, "Phantom of the Jungle," *Travel Holiday*, July-August 1999, p. 107.

8. Henry Walter Bates, *Naturalist on the Rivers Amazon.* New York: Humboldt Publishing Company, 1889, p. 230.

9. Interview with the author by telephone, May 2000.

10. Alan Rabinowitz, *Jaguar: One Man's Struggle to Establish the World's First Jaguar Preserve.* Washington, DC: Island Press, 2000, p. 195.

11. Quoted in Peter Friederici, "Return of the Jaguar," *National Wildlife,* June/July 1998. www.nwf.org/natlwild/1998/jaguar.html

12. Quoted in Friederici, "Return of the Jaguar."

13. Anne LaBastille, *Jaguar Totem.* Westport, NY: West of the Wind Publications, 1999, p. 223.

14. Rabinowitz, *Jaguar*, p. 310.

15. Quoted in Friederici, "Return of the Jaguar."

Chapter 2: Hunting the Jaguar

16. Roosevelt, *Through the Brazilian Wilderness*, pp. 78, 79.

17. Sasha Siemel, *Tigrero!* New York: Prentice-Hall, 1953, p. 89.

18. Tom Brakefield, *Big Cats: Kingdom of Might*. Stillwater, MN: Voyageur Press, 1993, p. 108.

19. Kristin Nowell and Peter Jackson, *Wild Cats: Status Survey and Conservation Action Plan*. Gland, Switzerland: The International Union for Conservation of Nature and Natural Resources, 1996, p. 220.

20. Nowell and Jackson, *Wild Cats*, p. 225.

21. Quoted in Lucien O. Chauvin, "Trafficking in Wild Animals Illegal, but Common in Peru," *Arizona Republic*, August 29, 1997, p. A14.

22. Interview with the author by telephone, April 2000.

23. Environmental News Network, "Venezuela Urged to Reconsider Jaguar Export Plan," May 21, 1997. www.enn.com/enn-news-archive/1997/05/052197/05219712.asp.

24. Wendell G. Swank and James G. Teer, "World Status of Jaguar, 1987," *Cat News*. http://lynx.uio.no/lynx/catfolk/cnissues/cn09-03.htm.

Chapter 3: Destruction of the Jaguar's Habitat

25. Edward O. Wilson, *The Diversity of Life*. New York: W. W. Norton, 1992, p. 333.

26. Quoted in Sharon Guynup, "Pristine Belize Threatened by Dam Plan," Environmental News Service. http://ens.lycos.com/ens/apr99/1999L-04-05-01.html.

27. Macal River Chalillo Project (press release). www.chalillobelize.org/press/press-11.html.

28. Quoted in Jeff Donn, "Amazon Forest Fading," Associated Press, April 8, 1999. http://forests.org/archive.brazil/amforfad.txt.

29. Andrew Taber et al., "The Food Habits of Sympatric Jaguar and Puma in the Paraguayan Chaco," *Biotropica 29 (2)*, 1997.

30. Nowell and Jackson, *Wild Cats*, p. 191.

31. Maurice Hornocker, "Can Cats Survive?" *Wildlife Conservation*, May/June 1996, p. 60.

Chapter 4: Jaguars in Zoos: Ambassadors to the Wild

32. Interview with the author by telephone, May 5, 2000.
33. Interview with the author by telephone, May 5, 2000.
34. Interview with the author by telephone, May 9, 2000.
35. Interview with the author by telephone, May 5, 2000.
36. Interview with the author by telephone, May 9, 2000.
37. Vicki Croke, *The Modern Ark*. New York: Scribner, 1997, p. 156.
38. Interview with the author by telephone, May 5, 2000.
39. Interview with the author by telephone, May 9, 2000.
40. Interview with the author by telephone, May 5, 2000.
41. Interview with the author by telephone, May 9, 2000.
42. Nowell and Jackson, *Wild Cats,* p. 270.
43. Interview with the author by telephone, May 5, 2000.
44. Croke, *The Modern Ark*, p. 19.
45. Interview with the author by telephone, May 5, 2000.
46. Interview with the author by telephone, May 23, 2000.
47. Interview with the author by telephone, May 9, 2000.

Chapter 5: Saving the Jaguar

48. Rabinowitz, *Jaguar*, p. 292.
49. Wildlife Conservation Society (fact sheet), Jaguar Research Projects. www.savethejaguar.com/res-brazilsur.html.
50. Interview with the author by telephone, June 6, 2000.
51. Interview with the author by telephone, May 9, 2000.
52. Wildlife Conservation Society (fact sheet), Jaguar Research Projects.
53. Wildlife Conservation Society (fact sheet), Jaguar Research Projects. www.savethejaguar.com/news-reports.html.
54. Wildlife Conservation Society, "Jaguar Helping Jaguars." www.savethejaguar.com/news-jaghelp.html.
55. Wildlife Conservation Society, "A Battle to Win: Jaguars," *New York Times*, January 9, 2000, p. 19.
56. Interview with the author by telephone, June 6, 2000.
57. Aldo Leopold, *A Sand County Almanac*. New York: Ballantine Books, 1984, pp. 151–52.

58. Quoted in Arnold, "In Belize, a Hunter Turns Protector," p. 2.

59. E.W. Sanderson, et al., "A Geographic Analysis of the Status and Distribution of Jaguars Across the Range," manuscript submitted for publication in *El Jaguar en el nuevo milenio*, Universidad Nacional Autonoma de Mexico/Wildlife Conservation Society.

60. Interview with the author by telephone, May 5, 2000.

Glossary

biodiversity: the existence of a variety of plant and animal life in a particular habitat or the world.

biosphere reserves: Protected natural areas designed to be large enough to maintain viable populations of plants and animals.

carnivore: An animal that eats the flesh of other animals.

CITES: Convention on International Trade in Endangered Species, an international treaty to protect animals and plants from commercial exploitation.

conservation: The managing and protection of the natural world.

deforestation: The removal of a large number of trees from an area.

ecology: The scientific study of the interaction of organisms with their environment and other organisms.

ecosystem: A community of interacting organisms and their physical environment.

endangered species: A type of plant or animal that is threatened with extinction.

extinction: A species is extinct when no living members exist.

extirpation: Disappearance of a species from a local area.

habitat: The natural area where a plant or animal lives.

IUCN: International Union for the Conservation of Nature and Natural Resources, known as the World Conservation Union, is an organization of about six hundred governmental and nongovernmental groups representing 116 countries with the goal to protect endangered and threatened living resources. Publishes "Red List" of endangered and threatened species.

nocturnal: Active at night.

poaching: Illegally hunting or capturing protected animals or plants.

predator: An animal that preys on other animals.

prey: An animal that is hunted for food by other animals.

radiotelemetry: Using radio collars to track animals in the wild.

rain forest: A dense evergreen forest with an annual rainfall of at least one hundred inches.

range: The area naturally occupied by a species.

reintroduce: To place members of a species in their original habitat.

reserve: An area of land set aside for the use or protection of a species or group of species.

species: A population of plants or animals distinguished from other such populations by certain characteristics.

Species Survival Plan: Captive-breeding programs administered by the American Zoo and Aquarium Association.

stalk: To hunt by moving slowly and quietly toward prey.

territory: The home area defined by the animal that lives within it.

vulnerable: A species that is at risk but not yet endangered.

wetland: A permanently moist lowland area such as a marsh or swamp.

Organizations to Contact

The Cat Specialist Group
Species Survival Commission
IUCN-The World Conservation Union
Rue Mauverney 28
1196 Gland
Switzerland
website: http://lynx.uio.no/catfolk/

This group of international cat experts and advocates offers information and facts about wild cats and wild cat conservation.

Cat Survival Trust
Marlind Centre
Codicote Rd.
Welwyn
Hertfordshire
AL6 9TV England
website: http://members.aol.com/cattrust

Dedicated to the conservation and rescue of wild cats, this organization provides care for captive cats and funds wild cat conservation.

Conservation International
2501 M St., NW, Suite 200
Washington, DC 20036
(202) 429-5660
website: www.conservation.org

This organization preserves and promotes awareness about the world's most endangered ecosystems through scientific programs, local awareness campaigns, and economic initiatives.

Defenders of Wildlife

1244 19th St., NW
Washington, DC 20036
(202) 659-4510
website: www.defenders.org

Since 1947, Defenders of Wildlife has advocated for ways to protect native wild animals and plants in their natural habitats. Focus is on the accelerated rate of species extinction and loss of habitat. The organization also serves as an information resource on endangered species.

Rainforest Action Network

450 Sansone, Suite 700
San Francisco, CA 94111
(415) 398-4404
website: www.ran.org

This grassroots organization works to protect the rain forests of the world and support rights of indigenous people through education, grassroots organizing, and nonviolent direct action.

Wildlife Conservation Society

2300 Southern Blvd.
New York, NY 10460
(718) 367-1010
website: www.wcs.org

Founded in 1895 as the New York Zoological Society, the WCS, headquartered in New York City's Bronx Zoo, works to save wildlife and wild places. The society runs five zoos and aquariums in New York City and supports field research around the world. A pioneer in environmental education and efforts to sustain biological diversity, the WCS's International Conservation program has many projects worldwide. In 1999, the WCS launched its jaguar conservation project.

World Wide Fund for Nature (WWF)
1250 24th St., NW
Washington, DC 20037
(202) 293-4800
website: www.wwf.org
This independent conservation organization has 4.7 million
supporters and a network in one hundred countries. WWF
works in countries around the world to conserve genetic,
species, and ecosystem diversity and to protect natural areas.

Suggestions for Further Reading

David Alderton, *Wild Cats of the World*, New York: Facts on File, 1993. An encyclopedic reference on wild cats.

Tom Brakefield, *Big Cats: Kingdom of Might*, Stillwater, MN: Voyageur Press, 1993. Beautiful photographs and well-researched essays, with lots of good facts, about the world's big cats.

Warner Glenn, *Eyes of Fire: Encounter with a Borderlands Jaguar*, El Paso, TX, Printing Corner Press, 1996. A photographic essay about an Arizona rancher's unusual experience with a jaguar.

Cathy Newman, "Cats: Nature's Masterwork," *National Geographic*, June 1997.

Barbara Sleeper, *Wild Cats of the World*, New York: Crown Publishers, 1995. An excellent reference book on wild cats.

Alan Turner and Mauricio Anton, *The Big Cats*, New York: Columbia University Press, 1997. Another good reference book on the jaguar, lion, tiger, and leopard.

Websites

Big Cats Online http://dialspace.dial.pipex.com/agarman. A comprehensive site on the tiger, lion, leopard, and jaguar. Offers excellent photographs and scientific and ecological information on the jaguar.

Cats www.nationalgeographic.com/cats. The *National Geographic's* website on the physical and behavioral characteristics of cats. Lots of interesting information.

Cats! Wild to Mild www.lam.mus.ca.us./cats/. Brimming with facts and figures about all cats, this site is based on a major cat exhibit at the Natural History Museum of Los Angeles County. Offers many links to cat-related websites.

Cockscomb Basin Wildlife Sanctuary www.belizeaudubon. org/html/parks/cbws.html. A description of the world's only jaguar reserve, located in the Maya Mountains of Belize in Central America. Also provides a look at the animals that share the jaguar's habitat.

Feline Conservation Center www.cathouse-fcc.org. The Exotic Feline Breeding Compound's Feline Conservation Center in Rosamond, CA, offers lots of information about the world's endangered wild felines and photographs of wild cats, including young jaguars born at the center's Cat House.

Save the Jaguar www.savethejaguar.com. The Wildlife Conservation Society's excellent website on jaguars and scientists' current efforts to preserve the jaguar's habitat and prey to allow it to survive in the wild.

Sierra Endangered Cat Haven http://www.cathaven.com. Good information on wild cats both in captivity and in their natural habitats. See the site's page on jaguars.

Works Consulted

Books

Henry Walter Bates, *Naturalist on the Rivers Amazon*. New York: Humboldt Publishing Company, 1889. The story of the British naturalist's historic nineteenth-century trip down the Amazon.

John A. Burton, ed., *The Atlas of Endangered Species*, 2d edition. New York: Macmillan Library Reference, 1999. A catalogue of the causes and extent of the worldwide endangerment of plants and animals.

Vicki Croke, *The Modern Ark*. New York: Scribner, 1997. The history of zoos and a look at controversial issues facing zoos today.

Lawrence Finsen and Susan Finsen, *The Animal Rights Movement in America: From Compassion to Respect*. New York: Twayne Publishers, 1994. An overview of the animal rights movement, including anti-fur campaigns.

Anne LaBastille, *Jaguar Totem*, Westport, NY: West of the Wind Publications, 1999. The first-person story of the adventures of a conservationist in Latin America.

Aldo Leopold, *A Sand County Almanac*. New York: Ballantine Books, 1984. The pioneering conservationist talks about his search for the jaguar and other endangered and extinct species.

Kristin Nowell and Peter Jackson, *Wild Cats: Status Survey and Conservation Action Plan*. Gland, Switzerland: The International Union for Conservation of Nature and Natural Resources, 1996. A comprehensive look at the status of wild cats and proposals to help save them.

Richard Perry, *The World of the Jaguar.* New York: Taplinger Publishing, 1970. A classic history of the jaguar in Latin America, with many colorful anecdotes of jaguar hunting and Indian jaguar lore.

Alan Rabinowitz, *Jaguar: One Man's Struggle to Establish the World's First Jaguar Reserve.* Washington, DC: Island Press, 2000. The first-person narrative of a young scientist who went to Belize to study jaguars and ended up saving them.

Theodore Roosevelt, *Through the Brazilian Wilderness.* New York: Charles Scribner's Sons, 1914. The U.S. president, naturalist, and big game hunter describes his experience in the jungles of Brazil, including his hunt for the jaguar.

Sasha Siemel, *Tigrero!* New York: Prentice-Hall, 1953. A famous jaguar hunter discusses his experiences stalking the big cat.

Don E. Wilson and Sue Ruff, ed., *The Smithsonian Book of North American Mammals.* Washington, DC and London: Smithsonian Institute Press, 1999. An excellent resource on mammals in North America, including a look at the jaguar.

Edward O. Wilson, *The Diversity of Life.* New York: W. W. Norton, 1992. The renowned zoologist tells how life on earth evolved and what the loss of biodiversity means, while he urges the rescuing of entire ecosystems, not just individual species.

Periodicals

David Arnold, "In Belize, a Hunter Turns Protector," *Boston Globe*, March 20, 1989.

Associated Press, "Two Get Prison, Fines for Selling Wild Cats' Fur," *Miami Herald*, November 27, 1998.

Gordon Chaplin, "El Tigre Hombre," *Audubon*, July 1985.

Lucien O. Chauvin, "Trafficking in Wild Animals Illegal, but Common in Peru," *Arizona Republic*, August 29, 1997.

William Conway, "Living with Cats," *Wildlife Conservation*, May/June 1996.

Maurice Hornocker, "Can Cats Survive?" *Wildlife Conservation*, May/June 1996.

K. Ullas Karanth, "Cat Scats and Other Telltale Signs," *Wildlife Conservation*, May/June 1996.

Dan Koeppel, "Phantom of the Jungle," *Travel Holiday*, July/August 1999.

Les Line, "Scientist at Work: Alan Rabinowitz: Indiana Jones Meets His Match in Burma." *New York Times*, August 3, 1999.

Loren McIntyre, "The Amazon—Mightiest of Rivers," *National Geographic*, October 1972.

Nancy Neff, "Cat Kin," *Wildlife Conservation*, May/June 1996.

Alan Rabinowitz, "Spirit of the Jaguar," *Wildlife Conservation*, May/June 1996.

E.W. Sanderson, et al., "A Geographic Analysis of the Status and Distribution of Jaguars across the Range," manuscript submitted for publication in *El Jaguar en el nuevo milenio*, Universidad Nacional Autonoma de Mexico/Wildlife Conservation Society.

Connie Cone Sexton, "Jaguar Twins to Go on Road," *Arizona Republic*, September 18, 1998.

Fiona Sunquist, "Power Cat: The Jaguar's Strength Is Awesome," *National Geographic World*, April 1998.

Andrew Taber, et al. "The Food Habits of Sympatric Jaguar and Puma in the Paraguayan Chaco," *Biotropica 29(2)*, 1997.

Wildlife Conservation Society, "A Battle to Win: Jaguars," *New York Times,* January 9, 2000, p. 19.

Internet Sources

Big Cats Online (fact sheet), "The History of the Wild Cats." http://dialspace.dial.pipex.com/agarman/bco1b.htm.

Julio Cesar Centena, "The Cry of the Jaguar." http://csf.colorado.edu/elan/jun97/0062.html.

Defenders of Wildlife (fact sheet), "Curbing the Wildlife Trade." www.defenders.org/defenders/citart.html.

Jeff Donn, "Amazon Forest Fading," Associated Press, April 8, 1999. http://forests.org/archive.brazil/amforfad.txt.

EFBC's Feline Conservation Center (fact sheet), "Enrichment." www.cathouse-fcc.org/enrich.html.

Katherine Ellison, "Brazil's Animal Trade Under Fire," *Miami Herald*, August 23, 1999. http://forests.org/archive/brazil/brantrad.htm.

Environmental News Network, "Cat Expert Applauds Listing of Jaguar as Endangered," July 23, 1997. www.enn.com/enn-news-archive/1997/07/072397/07239711.asp.

Environmental News Network, "Venezuela Urged to Reconsider Jaguar Export Plan," May 21, 1997. www.enn.com/enn-news-archive/1997/05/052197/05219712.asp.

Exotic Feline Breeding Compound's Feline Conservation Center (newsletter), *Spots 'N Stripes*, December 1999. www.cathouse.fcc.org.

Peter Friederici, "Return of the Jaguar," *National Wildlife*, June/July 1998. www.nwf.org/natlwild/1998/jaguar.html.

Sharon Guynup, "Pristine Belize Threatened by Dam Plan," Environmental News Service. http://ens.lycos.com/ens/apr99/1999L-04-05-01.html.

Jaguar Cars, "CC. Classics N.V., Exclusive Classic Cars, Jaguar." http://users/bart.nl/%7Eclassics/jaguar.html.

Macal River Chalillo Project (press release). www.chalillobelize.org/press/press-11.html.

Rainforest Action Network (fact sheet), "Oxy Invades Candoshi Homeland in Peru." www.ran.org/ran/info_center/aa/aa111.html.

Rainforest Action Network (fact sheet), "Species Extinction." www.ran.org/ran/info_center/factsheets/03b.html.

San Diego Zoo (fact sheet), "Paraguay's Chaco Region." www.sandiegozoo.org/cres/chaco.htm.

Sierra Endangered Cat Haven (fact sheet), "Cats of the Chaco 2000." www.cathaven.com/projectsurvival/chaco/chaco2000/catsofthechaco2000.htm.

Wendell G. Swank and James G. Tear, "World Status of Jaguar, 1987," *Cat News*. http://lynx.vio.no/lynx/catfolk/cn issues/cn09-03.htm.

Marcela Valente, "Environment—Argentina: Wildlife Tracked via Satellite," Global Information Network, Environment Bulletin, December 23, 1999. http://web2.infotrac.galegroup.com...582&dyn=4!xrn_2_0_A5842582&bkm_5_).

United Nations Population Division, "Revision of the World Population Estimates and Projections 1998." www.popin.org/pop1998.

Lily Whiteman, "Violence, Lies, and Videotape," *E/The Environmental Magazine*, May/June 1997. www.emagazine.com/may-june_1997/0597curr_3.html.

Wildlife Conservation Society (fact sheet), Jaguar Research Projects, Brazil. www.savethejaguar.com/res-brazilsur.html.

Wildlife Conservation Society (fact sheet), Jaguar Research Projects, Costa Rica. www.savethejaguar.com/res-costarica.html.

Wildlife Conservation Society, "Jaguar Helping Jaguars." www.savethejaguar.com/news-jaghelp.html.

Wildlife Conservation Society (fact sheet), Jaguar Research Projects. www.savethejaguar.com/newsreports.html.

World Conservation Monitoring Centre (fact sheet), "Darien National Park." www.wcmc.org/uk/protected_areas/data/wh/darien.html.

World Wide Fund for Nature (fact sheet), "WWF's Latin America & Caribbean Programme." www.panda.org/resources/inthefield/latin.

World Wide Fund for Nature (fact sheet), "Flora-Spotted Jaguar." www.wwf.org.br/wwfeng/evff04.htm.

World Wide Fund for Nature (fact sheet), "Conservation of Biodiversity in the Pantanal." www.wwf.org.br/wwfeng/wwfpr36.htm.

Dorothy Zimmerman, "Diplomacy in the Forest," World Wildlife Fund feature. www.panda.org/news/features/10-97/story4.htm.

Websites

American Museum of Natural History www.amnh.org. The museum's website has information on biodiversity and species extinction.

American Zoo and Aquarium Association (AZA) http://Aza.org. The AZA is the accrediting organization of North American zoos and wildlife centers.

Arizona Fish and Game Department's Jaguar Page www.gf.state.azus/frames/fishwild/jaguar.htm. Arizona's wildlife department examines jaguars and jaguar conservation in the Southwest.

AZA's Jaguar Species Survival Plan www.csew.com/felidtag/. This site explains the Species Survival Plan, which enables zoos in North America to coordinate their work in saving species.

Audubon Institute www.auduboninstitute.org. The Audubon Institute's Audubon Zoo in New Orleans has a Mayan rain forest exhibit with jaguars.

Belize National Parks, National Reserves and Wildlife Sanctuaries http://ambergriscaye.com/pages/town/parkcockscomb.html.

The Cat Specialist Group of the World Conservation Union (IUCN) http://lynx.uio.no/catfolk/onca-01. This international group of cat experts offers information about the jaguar and conservation of other wild cats.

Conservation International www.conservation.org. This organization conducts many wildlife and habitat conservation projects worldwide.

Convention on International Trade in Endangered Species www.cites.org/CITES/eng/index.shtml. This is a good place to find out more about the treaty protecting jaguars from international trade.

The Cyber Zoomobile www.priment.com/~brendel/jaguar.html. This comprehensive site on animals offers a detailed look at the jaguar.

Forest Conservation Archives http://forests.org/archive. Good resources with access to the latest news about rain forests and biodiversity.

Los Angeles County Museum exhibit—"Cats: Wild to Mild" www.lam.mus.ca.us/nhm. The recent exhibit on cats by the museum is full of interesting facts about wild cats, including jaguars.

Rainforest Action Network www.ran.org. This activist organization is a good source of facts about the rain forest.

Safari Club International www.safariclub.org. Nonprofit organization dedicated to conserving wildlife, educating the public, and protecting hunters' rights.

San Diego Zoo www.sandiegozoo.org. The San Diego Zoo is a pioneer in species survival and captive breeding of zoo animals.

U.S. Fish and Wildlife Service, Final Rule on the U.S. Population of Jaguars http://endangered.fws.gov/r/fr97622.html. A comprehensive look at the U.S. population of jaguars historically and at present.

Wildlife Conservation Society's Jaguar Conservation Program www.savethejaguar.com/newmillen.html. This site offers in-depth information on the current status of the jaguar in Latin America and scientific projects underway to save the species.

World Conservation Monitoring Centre www.wcmc. org.uk. A look at worldwide conservation programs, many of them in jaguar territory in Latin America.

World Resources Institute www.wri.org. The research and advocacy organization provides information, ideas, and solutions on global environmental problems.

World Wide Fund for Nature www.wwf.org and www.panda.org. This international organization has lots of information about projects underway to save wildlife species and wild places in Latin America.

Index

Picture Credits

About the Author

The Jaguar is Ann Malaspina's third book for Lucent Books. She wrote *Children's Rights* (1998) and *Saving the American Wilderness* (1999). She has a B.A. in English from Kenyon College and an M.S. in Journalism from Boston University. A former newspaper reporter with an interest in Latin America and environmental issues, she lives with her family in northern New Jersey.